There was a fisherman in China who for forty years used a straight needle to fish with. When someone asked him, "Why don't you use a bent hook?" The fisherman replied, "You can catch ordinary fish with a bent hook, but I will catch a great fish with my straight needle."

Word of this came to the ear of the Emperor, so he went to see this fool of a fisherman for himself. The Emperor asked the fisherman, "What are you fishing for?"

The fisherman said, "I am fishing for you, Emperor!"

If you have no experience in fishing with the straight needle, you cannot understand this story. Simply, I am holding my arms on my breast. Like that fisherman with the straight needle, I fish for you good fishes. I do not circulate letters. I do not advertise. I do not ask you to come. I do not ask you to stay. I do not entertain you. You come, and I am living my own life.

—Sokei-an

# ZEN PIVOTS

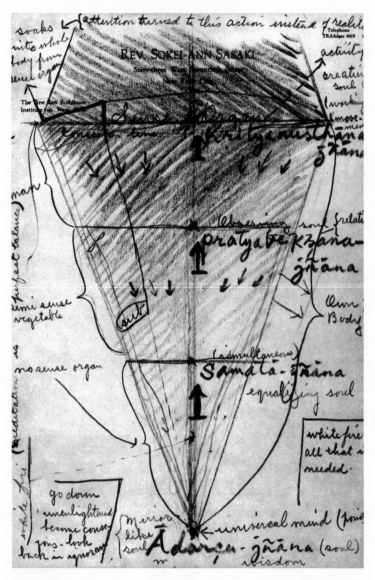

This diagram by Sokei-an represents the evolution of consciousness from its birth in the primordial sea of ignorance to its transformation by enlightenment into the wisdom of the Buddha. See "The Four Wisdoms" in this volume.

# ZEN PIVOTS

## Lectures on Buddhism and Zen

by

## SOKEI-AN

Edited by Mary Farkas & Robert Lopez

WEATHERHILL
New York & Tokyo

First edition, 1998

Published by Weatherhill, Inc., 568 Broadway, Suite 705, New York, NY 10012

Library of Congress Cataloging-in-Publication Data

Sasaki, Shigetsu, 1882–1945
    Zen Pivots: Lectures on Buddhism and Zen / by Sokei-an; edited by Mary Farkas and Robert Lopez. —1st ed.
      p.  cm.
    ISBN 0-8348-0416-6
    1. Zen Buddhism. 2. Religious life—Zen Buddhism. I. Farkas, Mary, 1910–1992.
II. Lopez, Robert. III. Title.
BQ9266.S266 1998
294.3'927—dc21                                      97-51894
                                                    CIP

*For Audrey Kepner, Edna Kenton, and Mary Farkas*

# CONTENTS

# BY WAY OF AN INTRODUCTION

*by Robert Lopez*

H ad she lived, the task of writing the introduction to this second
compilation of lectures by Zen Master Sokei-an would have fall-
en to his long-time editor and Zen student Mary Farkas. She, along
with Edna Kenton, Audrey Kepner and other early students and
friends of Sokei-an notated and preserved hundreds of lectures he
gave in English during the 1930s and 1940s at what he at times referred
to as the "Hermitage of Sokei," after the site of the Sixth Patriarch's
temple. At the request of its first members, Sokei-an founded his
Manhattan temple in 1930 as The Buddhist Society of America. In
1945, shortly before his death, the Society re-incorporated under the
name Sokei-an had originally wanted for the organization—The First
Zen Institute of America.

Mary, a small, impish woman, passed away in June 1992 at the
age of 81, leaving it to us at the Institute to complete the work she
began in 1938 when she became, as Sokei-an put it, a "pillar" of his
temple. When Sokei-an gave her the name Enen upon her initiation into the Buddhist *sangha*, he was calling forth the vigorous spirit of the compiler of the *Record of Lin-chi* [1], San-sheng Hui-jan (J.
Sancho Enen, n.d.)—a fitting appellation for the woman who
would for over fifty years devote her life to the task of delivering his
legacy into our hands.

In the weeks before Mary's death, many of us at the Institute spent
much of our time in the "abbot's" quarters, sitting beside her on the
wooden palanquin she called her bed. Her room, which was back of
the Institute's office, led to a garden of towering bamboo, and in the
years before her death she would often be found wandering about the
cathedral of grass in intimate conversation with the energetic and
vital life about her.

Mary's modest quarters had an equally tiny bathroom, a small closet, some bookshelves, a bed, and the detritus of past decades. On a dresser by the window stood Sokei-an's sculptures, among other knickknacks and personal memorabilia. A photo of Antony Tudor, her dearest friend, was mounted on the wall. Tudor had been principal choreographer for American Ballet Theatre and past president of the Institute before his death in 1987. Another photo of her husband, Nicholas Farkas, sat on the bookshelf above her bed, and at the entrance to her room was the death mask of Sokei-an, "demonstrating his nirvana," as she was wont to say.

Mary, suffering from the effects of a rare form of brain cancer, first lost the ability to move about in her usual graceful manner, then endured the physical torment of being confined to bed. She refused to be moved to more comfortable quarters, desiring to remain in this home she created after the death of her husband years before. In the dim light of her room she would talk softly of Sokei-an and the Institute. During one evening's conversation about the future publication of Sokei-an's commentary on the *Platform Sutra of the Sixth Patriarch*, she turned to me and said: "You know, don't you, we are not only presenting the *Sutra of the Sixth Patriarch* but the *Sutra of Sokei-an*—presenting the teaching of Sokei-an to the world. It's all here."

A splendid notion. Nevertheless, she did not live to see the completion of her work, so we must do without her words, and to my sorrow, without her.

As Mary grew increasingly aware of her age, she became preoccupied with ensuring that her work would be carried on by the Institute's members; and, as I had assisted her for several years preparing the Institute's periodical, *Zen Notes*, editing the *Sixth Patriarch* manuscript, and working on Sokei-an's first book, *The Zen Eye* (New York: Weatherhill, 1993), she asked me to continue with the effort she had begun so many decades before—that of getting Sokei-an into print. So, in accordance with her wishes, I have taken it upon myself to write this introduction to the lectures of Mary's beloved teacher.

S okei-an Shigetsu Sasaki was born in the old Japanese province of Sanuki on March 15, 1882, the son of a samurai, Tsunamichi Sasaki. Once a retainer of the Takamatsu clan, Tsunamichi became a successful Shinto scholar, teacher, and "missionary" during the Meiji period (1868–1912). Tsunamichi and his wife, Kitako Kubota, named their son Yeita. Yeita, however, was not the biological son of Kitako. His actual mother was said to be a concubine named Chiyoko. Ruth Fuller Everett, who would later become Sokei-an's second wife [2], describes the family situation at the time in some notes about his life.

> [Chiyoko] was the daughter of a tea master in Osaka and was sixteen or seventeen when she was taken as a temporary concubine by Sokei-an's father. Arrangements were made for his wife to retire and the temporary concubine remained until a son was born. After about two years she was returned to her family with a dowry. She married twice and had three or four children.
>
> The family of Sokei-an's father resented this. His father's family were samurai of the Sasaki clan. At the time of the Meiji Restoration, when the samurai class was disbanded, each was given government bonds according to rank. On these bonds Sokei-an's father lived. However, as he had kept selling them there was not much left when he died. He seems to have intended that Sokei-an would have recourse to this money. The mother's family, the Kubotas, were a fine family. Legally, Sokei-an should have become the head when his father died. The Kubota family had a conference in which they took the mother back into the Kubota family and dissolved the Sasaki family.... His mother, when she died at 80 or so, sometime after 1928, still had $10,000. Sokei-an asked her to give this to his wife [Tome Sasaki], who had lived with her. She did this.

Yeita remained the family's only child.

Sokei-an attended the usual primary and middle schools. After his father's death in 1897, Sokei-an went to Yokohama and apprenticed himself to a craftsman who specialized in carvings of temple exteriors. The next year he walked through the mountain range known as the Japan Alps, supporting himself by putting into service the tools he had used as an apprentice. Traveling from one temple to another asking for restoration work, he earned about thirty-five cents a day. Later, Sokei-an returned to Tokyo and his widowed mother. It was then that he first met Chiyoko. Ruth describes their meeting.

*Sokei-an met his real mother for the first time when he was living with his father's wife in Tokyo. She was beautiful and young. He met her in Ueno Park. There they were bothered by the police who thought she was a prostitute who had accosted him. The mother's sister was a geisha mistress (this means she had five or six geishas under her) in Osaka. Probably she had been a geisha. She was married. Through her he became acquainted with the geisha world and its lingo, which is very specialized. Another sister was a Joruri singer, as was also her husband. Sokei-an studied with them. Joruri singing includes long poems to samisen accompaniment as well as accompanying puppets in Bunraku. Sokei-an wanted to go into vaudeville at the theatre where the aunt and uncle, very popular, were appearing. Somebody dared him to go on the stage. Permitted to put on an act before they arrived, he was dragged off by them. He visited the geisha house several times. They were very nice to him.*

In 1899 Sokei-an entered the Imperial Academy of Art in Tokyo, where he studied sculpture under the famous artist Takamura Koun (1852–1934). During holidays he worked in the post office. In April 1905, he graduated from the Academy and was immediately drafted into the Japanese Imperial Army. Serving as a corporal in the transportation corps during the Russo-Japanese War (1904–05), he drove a dynamite truck on the Manchurian front, an experience he would frequently refer to in his commentaries. Waiting for his discharge he started a theater for the soldiers, writing plays, painting scenery, and acting in the productions as well. In 1906 he was demobilized, and a few months later found himself following his Zen teacher to America.

In 1902, Sokei-an had begun to study with Zen Master Sokatsu Shaku (1870–1954) at the Ryomo Kyokai, the "Society for the Abandonment of Subjectivity and Objectivity," whose headquarters were located in Nippori on the outskirts of Tokyo. The Ryomo Kyokai had been founded in 1875 by the celebrated Rinzai Zen master Imakita Kosen (1816–92) for the establishment and practice of lay Zen. Sokatsu had been appointed head of Ryomo Kyokai on his return from a pilgrimage in South Asia by Kosen's senior heir and student, Soyen Shaku (1859–1919). Sokei-an describes what it was like for the students at Ryomo-an.

*At the time, the disciples of Sokatsu Shaku were, for the most part, university students and young doctors, with a sprinkling of members of the nobility. The farmhouses of Nippori village were favorite lodging places for the university students who came from all parts of Japan. The village itself was quiet, but not too far from the city universities, and the households of the farmers afforded both pleasant and inexpensive living.*

*In rain and snow, or in fine weather, at six o'clock in the morning we students were assembled waiting for the gate of Ryomo-an to open. Quietly, we would enter the temple and, sitting together in the big room, which served as our zendo, we would practice meditation after the fashion of the sodo or monastery monks. At seven o'clock sanzen, catechism, began. One by one we would enter our teacher's room to answer the koan, or Zen question, which he had previously given to each of us. After sanzen, we would quietly leave the temple, returning home for breakfast and then going to our nine o'clock classes at school. Sunday passed as other days, except that our* roshi, *our Zen teacher, gave a lecture, or* teisho, *which we were all expected to attend* [3].

Soyen Shaku, abbot of Engakuji in Kamakura, was well known for having visited the United States in 1893 as part of a delegation of Buddhists to the World Parliament of Religions in Chicago. When a friend of Sokei-an's, a sculptor named Unkyo Goto, introduced him to Soyen, Sokei-an was taken aback:

*The first moment of this interview, the Abbot's two shining eyes pierced my mind through and through. I stood in silence, aghast! The Abbot questioned me about what I wished to become. I replied, "I am studying art." "What art are you studying?" I am learning how to carve Buddhist statues." "Who is your teacher?" "Koun Takamura." He looked into my eyes again and said, "Carve a Buddha statue for me when you become a famous artist." And he gave us tea and cakes* [4].

Sokei-an boldly decided to carve a buddha for Soyen. But when Sokei-an brought it to him, Soyen threw it out his window into a pond. Sokei-an later said, "It seemed unkind, but it was not. He meant me to carve the Buddha in myself."

In the spring of 1905, at his teacher's urging Sokei-an married Tome Sasaki in a Buddhist ceremony. On September 8, 1906, Sokei-an arrived in the United States with his wife, Sokatsu, and a group of students Sokatsu hoped would form the nucleus of a Zen community on a small parcel of land he had purchased in Hayward, California. Sokatsu expected his community of students to cultivate the land and become self-sufficient. But when their first crop failed—Sokei-an said the neighboring farmers made fun of their produce—Sokei-an confronted Sokatsu on the practicality of using "monks, artists, and philosophers" in such an undertaking. An argument ensued and Sokei-an left the community.

After it became clear the Hayward settlement would not succeed, Sokatsu opened a Zen center on Sutter Street in San Francisco. Sokei-an was already in the city studying at the California Institute of Art with Richard Partington, a well-known portrait painter. Sokei-an went to Sokatsu and apologized for "rebelling against his plans." He then resumed his study with his teacher.

But Sokatsu's venture in San Francisco faltered as well, and in 1910 he returned to Japan with his disciples. Sokei-an said, "I was the only one left behind." Sokei-an remained in the United States for the rest of his life, apart from two return visits to his native Japan.

Sokei-an later recalled his feelings about Sokatsu's departure:

*When I lost my teacher (he went back to Japan), I was left alone in this country. I had no one to follow, and I began to meditate upon the five* skandhas.

Samsara—*I could not understand it! Then one day I took my dog to the beach; he barked at the waves as they rolled in on the beautiful ocean strand. I realized that all this was reflected in the mind of my dog; he felt it in the dog's* samsara—*and expressed it.*

*I meditated upon* samsara *for many months. I watched the autumn foliage leave the trees. One leaf on a treetop waved to me like a hand—"I am going away, I am going away. Good-bye—winter has come!"* Samsara [5].

That year a son, Shintaro, was born to Tome and Sokei-an in San Francisco, and when they moved to Seattle, several months later a daughter, Seiko, was born.

Sokei-an supported his family by repairing art with the wood-carving tools he had carried with him from Japan. In 1916, Tome, who was pregnant with a second daughter, Shihoko, returned to Japan with Shintaro and Seiko. Shintaro returned to the United States in 1929; Seiko in 1930. Seiko would later marry into the Japanese-American Inouye family. Neither Tome nor Shihoko would ever return to the United States. Sokei-an missed his family and would see the face of his son behind the top of every bush. According to Ruth:

> *The reasons for her [Tome's] return were several: she did not like America; she did not want her last child born in America; SA [Sokei-an] 's mother Kitako was getting older and wanted her daughter-in-law to come back to Japan to care for her in her old age. Kitako had some means inherited from her husband and could help support Tomeko and the children. Tomeko never returned to America, and she and SA never lived together again. When SA returned to Japan in 1919 and 1926, he spent most of his time at Ryomo-an. He never ceased sending Tomeko and the children money each month until World War II stopped communications [6].*

Following his family's departure, Sokei-an decided to leave San Francisco with the aim of seeing the United States. He was twenty-four years old and had a fiercely independent nature.

> *Alone in America, [without his teacher] I conceived the idea of going about the United States on foot. In February, 1911[7], I crossed the Shasta Mountains through the snow into Oregon. On the hillside of the Rogue River Valley was the farm of an old friend. He asked me to stay with him for awhile.*
>
> *Summer came with the month of May. I began again my practice of meditation. Every evening I used to walk along the riverbed to a rock chiseled by the current during thousands of years. Upon its flat surface I would practice meditation through the night, my dog at my side protecting me from the snakes. The rock is still there.*
>
> *For several years I led a wandering life, finally reaching the city of New York. My carving-tools, cherished from the age of*

*fifteen, provided me with a hand-to-mouth livelihood. One
day all of a sudden, I realized that I must see my teacher. I
packed up my things and in October, 1919, left New York* [8].

A more vivid account of the circumstances of Sokei-an's departure
for Japan was offered by Ruth.

*[Sokei-an] went to New York and lived in Greenwich Village
and got to know some of the poets of those days. He knew the
first of the Beat Poets, shall I say, [Maxwell] Bodenheim, and
another person he knew was [Aleister] Crowley. And while his
interest in Zen kept on, during this period he was finding out
a lot about life. And then in 1919, in the summer, on an awfully, awfully hot day in July, he was walking down the street and
suddenly in the street he saw the carcass of a dead horse, and
something happened to him psychologically and he went
straight home to his rooms and packed up his things and got
a ticket for Japan and went back to Sokatsu* [9].

On March 28, 1922, after an intense period of Zen study, Sokatsu
granted Sokei-an *inka*, a Zen master's seal of approval authenticating
a student's experience of realization. Returning to the United States
in September 1922, Sokei-an once again settled in New York City,
resuming his art restoration work. During this second stay in New
York, he began to give lectures on Buddhism for a Mr. Brown at the
Orientalia bookstore on East 58th Street, opposite the Plaza Hotel.

Four years later, summoned by Sokatsu, Sokei-an returned to
Japan and resumed his Zen study. Meanwhile, a committee of
American and Japanese Buddhists had sent a letter to Sokatsu formally requesting that Sokei-an be appointed a teacher for their group
in New York.

*We know the reputation of Shigetsu Sasaki Koji* [10] *who
once taught here and inspired enthusiasm among Japanese*

as well as American Buddhists, who were deeply impressed with his splendid teachings. His vast knowledge of English, Sanskrit, Chinese, and Japanese, coupled with his remarkable understanding of social conditions in this country, fit him for a return here in this capacity. May we then urge his visit to this country, even if only for a brief period, say, six or eight months, so that we could continue our study of Dharma with his invaluable aid? [11]

In his reply to the New York group in May 1928, Sokatsu wrote:

Shigetsu Koji will come to you not only as one of the officials of our Associated Temples, but also in the capacity of Reverend, and assume the responsibilities of opening the American Branch of the Ryomo Society [12].

In July 1928, Sokei-an received formal certification as a teacher and was sent as a representative of the Ryomo Society to the United States:

Under the guidance of a single teacher I had passed through the training of Zen from beginning to end. My Roshi (Zen Master) authorized me to promulgate Zen, saying, 'Your message is for America. Return there!' With the help of friends I came back to New York and began my work [13].

In August, when Sokei-an arrived in New York, the committee sent an ecstatic letter to Sokatsu thanking him and informing him of Sokei-an's arrival. But the New York group did not live up to its promise. Their interest had so seriously waned that after a short time Sokei-an left the group. Now and then, he said, he "busied himself preaching the Dharma in various quarters."

When [Sokei-an] went back again to New York in 1928, [Ruth Sasaki noted] he felt he was completely alone with nothing *but his Zen. His teacher had told him that now his life was to be devoted to teaching Zen and no more to earning his living by some other manner and toying with Zen on the side, and so at first he didn't know quite what to do. He didn't have any group to go to. He was more or less alone. He had a commission from some magazine or newspaper... to write a series of articles on the various foreign people who lived in New York City and made up its population [14]. So instead of going back to Greenwich Village and picking up that type of friend and acquaintance again, he lived for two or three months apiece with an Italian family, a Portuguese family, and eventually a Negro family—I don't know how many others—but the Negro family was the last, and then he was forced to do something to eat and he went to Mr. [Mataichi] Miya, of the Yamanaka [Company, dealers in antique furniture]. Whether he had known him previously, or how he got to know him I don't exactly know, but at any rate, Mr. Miya was very interested in Zen [and] had studied Zen previously, and so he gave Sokei-an $500 and went around and hunted for a place for him to live and to begin to give his lectures [15].*

At some time after he received his appointment from the Ryomo Society, Sokei-an decided that if he was to make any headway with Americans, it was essential he become a priest. He therefore, arranged to become a disciple of Master Aono Futetsu, abbot of Manmanji, a branch of the famous headquarters temple Daitokuji. On March 15, 1933, Sokei-an formally received the precepts and the rank of attendant (*jisha*) at Daitokuji, along with the religious name Soshin. All of this, through a complex but accepted procedure, was carried out while Sokei-an remained in New York.

Sokatsu would have preferred that Sokei-an remain a lay teacher. Indeed, Kosen and Sokatsu's original intention in creating and maintaining the Ryomo Society had been to establish a lineage based squarely on lay practice, represented by lay teachers. Sokei-an's ordination as a priest very much displeased Sokatsu and for a while ruptured their relationship.

On February 15, 1930, with the support of his many Japanese and American friends, Sokei-an finally opened the Buddhist Society of America at 63 West 70th Street, situated a block from one of his favorite New York City locales, Central Park.

A student described the temple rooms:

*Sokei-an's first-floor apartment [was in the] front, two rooms with kitchen and bath. The front room had a large bay window with hinged window seats for storage. It was an unusually long room with the bay giving added length. It could seat fifty when necessary—has seated even more. Folding doors separated it from the Zen room, which the audience faced. In 1935, Osho took them down, made four folds instead of two, and pasted them over with pages from the* Avatamsaka Sutra, *the epitome of which he was making ready to translate—the* Five Measures of the Meditation of the Avatamsaka Sect *by To-shun. He antiqued them, fitted them in place.... The wood fish drum had its place nearby.*

*Osho sat at a low comfortable reading table, facing the bay windows, as he lectured, surrounded by his books, a few pictures, now and then a mandala.*

*There was a fireplace, unused, on the west wall. On its mantle shelf was a small altar arrangement, where the "pebble-stone" was placed first, and later the image we bowed before.*[16]

*Later, because we accidentally discovered he had wanted it very much, Neil Reber arranged to have a small window cut through the north kitchen wall—a "monk's window" he could slide open and look into the hall when his bell was rung. It was unusual in a New York apartment, and it gave him much amusement to conduct what business he could through it.*

On the north wall of the lecture room—the living room—
hung a framed temple motto or whatever, in large, black
type: "Those who come are welcome. Those who go are not
pursued"....

He had a large window box on the eastern side of the bay
window, facing Central Park. It was no florist's dream. Once
he planted a potato and pondered its blossom. "The ancestor
of the Shakya tribe was a potato," he told us. "Means
Shakyamuni's ancestors were farmers." And always ivy was
somewhere about—a favorite figure of speech for the
intrinsic nature of man—"to seek the light, as the ivy in a
dark cellar stretches its little hands to the cold ray creeping
in through the cellar window."

He worked over his Zen room—the most precious space to
him in his home—embellishing it with brocades, changing
its lighting from time to time. His small altar there was very
lovely, with its lighted candles when its mysterious doors were
thrown open after sanzen. In that room it was eye to eye. [17]

In her decades-old never-completed running biography of Sokei-
an, Mary recalled her first meeting with him at the Buddhist Society:

One evening—it happened to be June 22, 1938—I entered a
room at the main floor front of 63 West 70th Street, New
York City.... Promptly at 8:30 a lady with large brimming
eyes reminiscent of a character in Swann's Way... took a
position at the reading desk and announced that Shramana
[18] Sokei-an Sasaki... would read a translation he had
made from the Sutra of the Sixth Patriarch of Zen in China
and comment upon it. Thereupon a rather large Japanese,
robed as a priest, entered through a pair of sutra-papered
doors at the north end of the room and performed a brief ceremony that included the burning of incense and chanting.
At its conclusion, he seated himself at a reading desk on

*which were, in addition to his manuscript written in red Chinese characters, a ceremonial fly-whisk, a crystal glass, and a curious scepterlike object with an involute top. We then observed a period of silence, during which he sat before us like an image on a mountaintop. To tell the truth, it was more like a mountain, if a man may be said to be like a mountain, in huge immobility* [19].

From 1929 until September 1941, 70th Street not only served as the headquarters of the Buddhist Society but as Sokei-an's place of residence [20]. Two to three evenings a week Sokei-an gave *sanzen* and then lectured in the traditional Zen manner. During the day, he worked on his translations, including the *Record of Lin-chi*, the *Platform Sutra*, and the *Sutra of Perfect Awakening*. He would also visit Central Park and go to the movies. Regarding his status and aims in presiding as teacher at the Society, Sokei-an said:

*For a Zen master there are three rules: 1) you shall not unpack your outfit—your trunk—however many years you live in that temple; 2) and you must hang your umbrella on the wall; 3) and you must keep your straw sandals ready.*

*I have unpacked, but for two years I did not unpack my trunk. There was a big reason. For the Buddhist monk must not give himself two powers: first, the power of gold—money power; second, the power of politics—government* [21].

But on December 7th, 1941, the day of the Japanese attack on Pearl Harbor, as the Society was moving into its new quarters at Ruth's home at 124 East 65th Street, Sokei-an came to the attention of this "government." Disaster loomed on the horizon for the Society and for Sokei-an. Ruth recalls those events:

*From that time on—of course for months we didn't know it—there were two FBI people under the present apartment verandah twenty-four hours a day. Mr. Sasaki was interviewed many times by the FBI, and so was I; but the meetings were permitted to be continued until June. On the 15th of June 1942, he gave his last talk; and the next day he was taken and was interned* [22].

After thirty-six years in the United States, Sokei-an was arrested as an "enemy alien" and sent to Ellis Island, New York. In October 1942, he was transferred to Fort Meade, an internment camp near Baltimore, Maryland. The articles about America written so many years before had returned to roost. Sokei-an would later admit in a letter to Ruth that "My hobby caused me to be here."

Sokei-an was shocked and disheartened by the actions of his adopted country. Many of the letters he sent from Ellis Island are heartbreaking—"The Island is shrouded in drizzling rain. Avalokitesvara weeps over me today…. I am waiting for Alice in the wonderland to come."

He would write every day to his friends and family, sending them his greetings, reminding those in Manhattan to tell Chaka, his cat, that he loved him, and that he would return. Edna Kenton visited Sokei-an on February 7, 1943, and in a letter to the "Girls"—Mary and other younger female members of the Institute—wrote about her meeting with Sokei-an in Maryland.

*Dear Girls,*
*This is a message from Osho—I went down last Sunday the 7th bearing gifts for his birthday—since we cannot see him next Sunday—and among a few messages he especially sent back, he said, "—and those children, to them my especial regards." He was looking very well, in his seal fur cap, his fur-collared windbreaker coat, and his new corduroy trousers, which, alas, though only a week old, I took for his old ones! so work-worn and stained and creased and pressed down they were. He is very busy, carving a "dragon cane" for the*

*Colonel—from a tall cedar stick—"'bout so long"—picked
up somewhere in the area and on which he has been working for several weeks—"will take 'bout ten days longer," he
said. I said before four soldiers that I hoped the Colonel
appreciated the value of what he was about to receive, a
wood carving from the hands of a graduate of the Royal
Academy of Tokyo, which put the Colonel in Mrs. John D.
Rockefeller's class—among others—who had some of his
carvings in her collection! The privilege of taking up his
wood carving, with whatever primitive tools, had done won-
ders for him; and the granting him a "studio"—one of the
unoccupied houses—where he and a few other artists down
there can work. I asked him if he was using the little red seated camp chair (you knew that Mabel carried down by hand
on January 19th one of the old Temple chairs?) and he
laughed and said; "I am sitting on that chair from morning
to evening!" Good luck [23].*

After spending close to a year in the Fort Meade internment
camp, Sokei-an was finally released by the government in August
1943, following a vigorous campaign mounted on his behalf by his
students. Sokei-an returned to Manhattan, and the following year he
traveled with Ruth Everett to Little Rock, Arkansas, to obtain a
divorce from his first wife, Tome, and to marry Ruth Fuller. Ruth
said, "SA had tried for many years to have a divorce arranged in
Japan, but Tomeko would not consent, even up to the time war was
declared [24]."

Sokei-an's arrest effectively ended his formal teaching career, but
he would continue to give *sanzen* until his death twenty-one months
later. On Thursday, May 17, 1945, suffering from a variety of compli-
cations due to high blood pressure, Sokei-an passed away at 6:00 P.M.
in his apartment on 65th Street, surrounded, as Ruth said, "by those
he loved and who loved him devotedly."

Shortly before his death, Sokei-an made a request of Mary:

*When Sokei-an overstayed his leave in this world according to his own calculations, that is, outlived the day he predicted for his own death, he asked me, somewhat jokingly, to give him a new name, as he said this was the custom. I racked my mind for a name for this great and wonderful person who was my teacher, warm and close as a member of my family from one point of view, remote as the final nirvana he was about to enter from another. Only one name came to my mind: "Tiger-heart." He accepted this as quite appropriate, and a few weeks later he was gone* [25].

Nine days before his death, on May 8th, the Allies declared Victory in Europe. On August 6th and 9th, Hiroshima and Nagasaki were destroyed by atomic blasts. Japan surrendered on the 14th — two hundred and forty thousand Japanese had been reduced to ashes. The total human cost of the World War II would approximate fifty-five million people. In "Compensation," a 1939 lecture included in this volume, Sokei-an conveys the terrible feelings of that time.

*I carry this message to the West. It is my mission. To give this message to America is my purpose. There are many philosophies in the West talking about Reality, but their message isn't complete. They never return from there. I brought this complete teaching from the East. Even in Japan many monks attain just one side. I began to study Zen at an early age. At forty-eight I completed the hairpin turn of Buddhism.*

*I came to America this last time in 1928, on August 16th, when I landed in Seattle, Washington. I have stayed ten years. On the first day I began to make a hermitage. Everyone helped me. Everyone fought against invisible enemies. Those who will be converted to Zen in the future are our enemies. We are fighting against them to capture them. Many have been wounded and dropped out of the lines, but all those people who helped have left mementos that are still vivid in this temple. Their footprints are everywhere and their bloodstains are left, and I am grateful to them.*

*I have reached the point where I have dug a trench and embanked it and made a foothold. I have worked for ten years, and my friends helped me, and I shall be working for another ten years. I am not doing this for my own purpose; I would be happier in Japan working with my own people. But I love this country, and have decided to die in this country. Eastern civilization must be brought here; we have been misunderstood. I shall die here, clearing up debris to sow seed. It is not the time for Zen yet. But I am the first of the Zen School to come to New York and bring the teaching. I will not see the end* [26].

F ew of Sokei-an's extemporaneous talks, lectures, and commentaries were written out by him. The notes taken by his students were to be left in their hands. In his commentary on the closing chapter of the *Platform Sutra*, Sokei-an said,

*I have been giving lectures on the Sixth Patriarch's record for about four years, and now there remain a few more weeks. Then this long translation will come to an end. I hope that after my death someone will publish this translation in a book for future Zen students.*

He left it to his students to create his "record," much as the Zen records of past masters were created by their disciples.

Every lecture he gave of which a record remains was recorded by hand by one or more of his students who were present. The notes were typed, and then typed once again, one under the other, very much like the text of a chorale or cantata, so that they would all coalesce into a seamless record of the evening's presentation, recreating Sokei-an's voice through a sort of common consent. The extraordinary thing about all of this is that he gave all his lectures in English.

In the early forties, however, Sokei-an did begin to write out a commentary on the *Record of Lin-chi* at the behest of Ruth Fuller Everett, and in 1940–41 he composed articles for his newsletter, *Cat's Yawn*, dealing with the history of his lineage and the particulars of Zen training. Besides the lectures he gave at the Buddhist Society, Sokei-an also spoke at other religious organizations and conferences in the Boston and New York areas, including the churches of Harlem.

In the early thirties, two of Sokei-an's longtime Zen students, Audrey Kepner and Edna Kenton, were the principal note-takers. Edna, whom Sokei-an said he "used like an old shoe," was a playwright and author, as well as the Buddhist Society's archivist, historian, and treasurer. Sokei-an named her "Iron-Mortar" after "Iron-Grinder" Liu, an old woman of Ch'an (Zen) [27]. Audrey Kepner, the recording secretary of the Society, was a retired high school history teacher who helped Sokei-an with his English and assisted him with his first major translation [28]. Audrey began studying with Sokei-an in 1930, Edna in 1933. Mary, sometime after her own arrival, joined the groups that met to compile and edit Sokei-an's lectures. The final versions of his talks were published by Mary in *Zen Notes* beginning in 1954. Mary wrote about this process in response to a query about how she prepared a Sokei-an article for her periodical.

> The notes were taken by a writer, Edna Kenton, and a school teacher, Audrey Kepner, whose major interest was comparative philosophy and religion. Their accuracy is judged three ways: by each other; by the facts ascertainable elsewhere; by agreement with statements made by Sokei-an on other occasions.
>
> Our first step is to try to find out what Sokei-an said. After a collation sheet is made, in this case from two persons, sometimes from more, a rough draft is made... It should be

*Sokei-an's actual words, as nearly as possible. His English was, of course, not English, but reading his actual words, as he habitually used them, in many different cases, gives a clearer sense of what he had in mind than a completely polished version of what anyone else believes he meant. It is therefore his sense I try to find, not just a sense. This can only be determined by acquaintance with his thinking* [29].

When Edna Kenton died in 1954 at the age of 78, Mary inherited her position as custodian of Sokei-an's legacy. Edna had doggedly safeguarded his lectures from the beginning of her career at 70th Street, but it was Mary who seized the opportunity of rescuing Sokei-an from his students' notebooks and began publishing the edited articles in *Zen Notes*.

Sokei-an's intention to personally introduce his students to the tenets of the Buddhist "canon," as he called it, through his weekly meetings made it imperative that he translate the selected materials himself. This he did from his complete edition of the Chinese Tripitaka, donated to the Buddhist Society in 1930 by an admirer and friend, Kazuo Kawazuchi. His lectures on various Buddhist topics, translations, and commentaries provided his American students with an authentic context for their faith as Buddhists; and his *sanzen*, the "face-to-face," or "mind-to-mind" encounter between master and student, provided them with the core of Zen itself—the perspective of what he called their "original aspect."

Sokei-an spoke in a natural manner, free of the pretension, ostentation, or artifice found in so much of Zen literature. He learned his English in the farmlands and cities of the West and the apartments of Harlem and Greenwich Village in the East. He would tell his students that he was "from Missouri" and had to be *shown* the answers to the koans he assigned them.

Sokei-an's talks are filled with the intimate details of his life in America and in his native Japan. He commented upon the triumphs and frailties of human nature in a profusion of anecdotes and tall tales of every variety. His examples, drawn from his own experiences with his family, friends, students, and teachers, as well as the turbaned gurus of the day, are told in a voice that is remarkably perceptive, delightfully frank, and clear as a bell.

> When I came to this country, I went to Mount Rainier and sat on the corner of a stone in a little village, thinking. A farmer came along and asked me, "What are you doing?"
> "I am thinking," I said,
> "Thinking spoils your head," he said.
> "Spoils my head! I've been thinking for twenty years! My head is spoiled completely!" [30]

The lectures that comprise *Zen Pivots* are Sokei-an's introduction to the theory and practice of Buddhism. As his students had no acquaintance with the structure Buddhists had created over a period of twenty-five hundred years to explain the development of consciousness and its awakening, he felt it was his responsibility to do so in as precise and methodical a manner as was possible considering the limitations imposed upon him by the circumstances of the situation. His students did not have the voluminous amounts of material available to them that we have today. The resources at hand were extremely limited, and much of it was heavily encased in the "mysticism" and "Oriental" tomfoolery of the "esoteric" or "occult" variety. In a comment on his particular method of lecturing, Sokei-an said:

> I beg your pardon for my slow speech but first I must think these things I am going to speak in my mind, then I must translate it into English, and then I must carry out the dharmakaya [31] *itself before your eyes, so naturally I cannot speak as I would read a book.*

For Sokei-an, the dignity and nobility of Buddhism and by extension, Zen, lies not in its magisterial constructs or in its richly intoxicating ritual, but in its utterly single-minded quest for the arousal from slumber of our "original" or "true" nature—in the very activity of living.

Sokei-an systematically taught on Buddhist philosophy, epistemology, psychology, and early Buddhist teachings in unsparingly difficult "series" of lectures that stretched over periods of months and years. He translated hundreds of Sanskrit terms and concepts from the Chinese and lectured on their significance in such series as "Primitive Buddhism," "Outline of Buddhism," "Terms of the Dharma," "Mahayana Buddhism," and the like. The lectures that comprise this volume are drawn from those talks.

This type of lecture is unusual for a Zen master. Soeki-an, however, was following in the footsteps of his teacher Sokatsu Shaku, who followed those of Soyen Shaku and Imakita Kosen. Their embrace of "primitive" Buddhism was in the hope of reviving Zen from the moribund state to which it had sunk in the temples of Japan, a Zen they felt had divorced itself from daily life. Their aim was to introduce to the new century a form of Zen unencumbered by the formalistic and ritualistic incrustations of the past. From this came their emphasis on lay practice and their "analytical," detailed questioning of (and meditation on) the tenets of early Buddhism.

After his teacher's departure in 1910, Sokei-an had been left in America to continue his studies on his own, and it was in this formative period that he examined his own mind in the light of the early Buddhist teachings. He succinctly explains the aim of this process in his commentary on the *Platform Sutra of the Sixth Patriarch*:

> *Bodhidharma's point is this: the sutras were written and the lectures were given to help us to awaken to Reality. But the sutras and lectures are not religion. They are the ferryboat to carry us to Reality. It is by handling reality that we awaken to the state of Reality, and that is action. It is the same sort of thing that you are using in your daily life.*

So when Sokei-an spoke on the theory and practice of Buddhism, he spoke from his own experience and from the Eye of Zen he had acquired in *sanzen*. He would have been very much surprised to hear, as we do these days, that Zen is meditation, stillness, mindfulness, breathing, tea, or baseball. For Sokei-an, Zen is simply the manifestation of *dharmakaya*, the actual, concrete realization of our original aspect that he characterized as Great Nature.

*In deep samadhi, when our own mind ceases to exist, our mind is switched to the Great Universe. Its rhythm is not coarse, like our usual thinking, but this state of nothingness is not dead; it is living. Then, for the first time, the individual ego makes contact with the Great Ego of the Universe, and the small ego surrenders before this Great Ego [32].*

The lectures in *Zen Pivots* are a fresh view of that old mystery—human awareness. Every one of these talks was given in gratitude and love from the first American Zen master.

*New York City*
*Spring 1998*

# ZEN PIVOTS

*I came here and I am preaching Buddhism. I did not intend to, but my teacher brought me to America when I was young. I studied my ABC's and went back to Japan to remain there. But somehow that Columbia River and that range of Rocky Mountains stuck in my dreams. Then I was asked to come here and I came.*

—Sokei-an

# PREFATORY REMARKS BY SOKEI-AN

I thought I would never repeat the same subject in a lecture, but I have a desire that someone shall carry on this teaching after my death. In order to show you in what way I have been thinking of Buddhism and in what attitude I have been carrying on this teaching, I must repeat the same subject again and again until you thoroughly understand the important pivots of my way of thinking.

In Japan a Zen master does not give this kind of lecture because there are many books written which students can read to gather their knowledge of Buddhism. But in this Western hemisphere I cannot recommend any book that is translated into English by your scholars. Of course, there are some translations which were not mistranslated from the original texts, but they always omit the most important pivots which must be emphasized in that translation in order to understand what is meant.

I shall leave three or four sutras translated by my own hand, and besides that, I shall tell you what way I am thinking about Buddhism, and this will be material on which you can rely to promulgate this teaching. Of course, when I open my mouth to speak about "popular" Buddhism, perhaps the words which I use to explain it will not be at all in the nature of popular Buddhism, though I shall try to make it as plain as possible. It is, however, very difficult to grasp the pivots of Buddhism.

# FREEDOM

I n my hometown I kept a canary in a cage. And as I was very keen about this canary, I made a cage of very strong wire because there were many weasels snitching chickens and eggs. The roof of the cage I made of straw. One evening I came home and found him holding a stick tightly in his beak with his eyes closed. I shook the cage and found that he was dead. I could visualize the weasel running around the cage sniffing and trying to pry open the wires, until the bird died of fear.

I think all beings long for freedom.

# DOUBT

I had the sickness of doubt in my youth. I could not read, study, or eat. I was shivering and pale. I was called "Grasshopper-legs" and "Blue-spike." Somehow I had to settle the question.

I was a spoiled child, who thought no one was like myself. I was that type of young man. It was not until after I was thirty-seven that I came into a world of some sunshine, where I could enjoy the outside and associate with friends. Before that I was ill-natured and quick-tempered. I really felt that the earth filled up my mind, and it was the end of joy [33]. If I could not pass my koan within a month, I was sick; I could not enjoy anything. Sometimes I wondered how anyone could live, and what would happen after death. Reincarnation was just talk. Transmigration was just talk. Karma was just talk. I had five senses, but how were they connected after death? What senses would stay, and what would go? So many questions. What was love? What was morality?

Then I settled from corner to corner. It was like peeling the skin of an orange. I did very careful work, very tedious work; otherwise, I thought, there was no use living. I am doing something very important, but will I starve to death? Even so, I had to get everything settled and come to terms with myself. Otherwise, I could not go on. It was like settling one's accounts at the end of the month. If you can't find the error, you can't sleep. The question of everyday life is the same. You must think deeply into it, for no one else's sake but for your own. Otherwise, your life is just nonsense. If I don't know what will happen after death, how can I lie down comfortably to die?

Heaven and hell—just talk. Angels and gods—just talk. Can I go to death believing such things? Life is a little more serious than that! If I am not clear about the conclusion of life, I cannot continue.

# FAITH

For each student of Buddhism there is always some gate through which to enter its main avenue. In true Buddhism, however, there is no gate open to the public with ushers standing on both sides, smiling and beckoning you to come in. The gate of true Buddhism is always closed. When you knock, no one will answer. So you must break in. Unless you do, you can only stand on the outside talking about it, but you yourself will never be admitted to see the beautiful treasures; you will have to wait for one who has returned from there to tell you about them.

But in Zen there is no gate, and no one can get in. There is a famous saying in Zen, "The Great Tao has no gate." Here, Tao means "Mind." Mind is the gate, and you do not need to enter; you are already inside. And you do not need to open the door; there is no door. And you do not need to break in, there is nothing to be broken. Just sit down with this Great Mind. The Mind itself is the Great Tao.

When the Sixth Patriarch [34] was being pursued by the monks that wanted the robe and bowl given to him by his teacher, the Fifth Patriarch, he placed them on a rock. Hui-ming, who had caught up with him, tried to lift them, but they were as heavy as a mountain, and they could not be moved. The Sixth Patriarch said to him, "Faith cannot be attained by force."

That faith is a good word. It is not necessary to believe anything, it is not necessary to have faith in God, or in the Devil, but there is something in the human mind which is the pivot of all consciousness, and we base all our attitudes upon it. There is something in human beings that is grand, that is penetrating and pure, that is sacred. It is not tinted by any color. It has no particle of sound, no taste. It is like air, and we feel it. It is faith. Faith is the residence of our religion.

# THE RELIGION OF NORTH AMERICA

To make clear the nature and significance of Buddhism, it is necessary to speak of Taoism. One must also make clear the distinction between Christianity and Buddhism. Then we can think about what the religion of North America might be like in the future.

I have been asked many times about Taoism, but I have not made any particular answer. Lao Tzu, who wrote the *Tao Te Ching*, left only five thousand words in all. His words are very simple and concise. Today, Tao is usually translated as "Way," but this is not a very good translation. Tao is Way; it is true, but it is also "emptiness," "naturalness," and "purposelessness."

Lao Tzu placed particular emphasis on purposelessness, in Chinese *wu-wei*, the cardinal principle throughout his five thousand words on the Tao. *Wu* means "no" or "not," and *wei* means "to do." So *wu-wei*, in Sanskrit, *asamskrita*, means "to do nothing," or "doing nothing [35]." In Taoism, however, this doing nothing has a special meaning. If someone asks, "What are you doing?" and you answer, "Nothing," that is not it. You are doing everything, but from the standpoint of the individual you are doing nothing. When you digest food, for instance, digesting food is not your doing, but you are still digesting food. When I walk the streets, my feet carry my body, but "I" am not walking.

If you do not understand this, you will never understand the Chinese. No one on earth can be so charming as a Chinese gentleman doing nothing from morning to evening. The sun rises in the morning and sets at night. Spring comes and flowers bloom. Fall comes and the trees shed their leaves. But the sun does nothing, and the trees do nothing. All these activities have no purpose. They are just phenomena.

In the old days, the entire life of the land of China was performed on this principle. No nation on earth worshipped Nature as the Chinese did. Purposelessness is natural and naturalness is emptiness. How could I speak about Taoism without talking about emptiness? Purposelessness, naturalness, emptiness—these are the three standards of Taoism.

Naturalness is like the love of a mother for her child. She is not expecting any reward. She enjoys giving, and there is no purpose in her giving. Sometimes we use the words "benevolence," "sympathy," "compassion," but these words describe attitudes toward outsiders. These attitudes are not as wonderful as the love a mother gives to her child. You may help someone and not expect a return, but it is not the same as when you help your own child. For when you help someone else, you are aware that you are helping; but when you help your own child, you are not aware of it.

And then there is duty. I was in the Japanese army for eight months when I was young. The officer gave orders, and I obeyed. Even if he ordered something impossible, I would reply, "Yes, sir!" His orders had no selfish motive, and I obeyed impersonally. But if I were working in a factory and the proprietor took advantage of me for his own purpose, and I would have to obey him as a slave, I would not call this duty. There is no Taoism then, no purposelessness, naturalness, or emptiness. Instead, there are strikes and trouble. When law is based on the Tao, everything moves and is natural. Unfortunately, it is theory I am speaking about. Today all is changing.

If I were to translate Tao into a Christian term, it would be "Love." Pure, disinterested, purposeless, natural love, the love between the Father and the Son. That is Tao, too, isn't it? With this Love, the Western world has had its civilization for two thousand years. It is the love of the Father, however. He is kind, but His love is not the same kindness as that of a mother for her child. In Buddhism we use the term Dharma, which can mean "law" or "religion [36]," but Dharma is nothing but Tao, or Love, too.

Taoism is China. Shinto is Japan. What will the religion of America be? This continent has rich soil, good climate, fat horses, and beautiful women. It is very different from the densely populated Europe it imitates. Yet, there are still open spaces in America's vast West, empty except for sagebrush, where you can ride for half a day and see only a few cows or prairie chickens. There is something of the greateartedness of the American Indian in its people's generosity. Tao is already here. Here, Christian Love and Chinese Tao meet.

I think of America like this: It could be the meeting ground for the religions of East and West. If Tao can be incorporated into the life of America, what a wonderful country it could be!

# IS THERE SOME BENEFIT
# FROM STUDYING BUDDHISM?

February 15th is my birthday [37]. I have reached sixty years in this human life, and I have been following the Buddha's teaching from my twentieth year. What have I gained from studying Buddhism for forty years? For about twenty years I thought I was greatly benefited by Buddhism, but in the last twenty years I have been ungaining everything I had learned. The conclusion, I would say, is that I have gained nothing. There have been many from ancient times who have asked this question. In the sutras it is asked, and answers have also been given. One answer was no, the other was yes.

One day while Ananda was standing beside the Buddha, fanning him, the Buddha asked him: "Is it going to rain today, or not? Do you think the monks can beg for food today in the town, or not?"

Ananda did not answer. Instead he left the place where the Buddha was and went among the monks. He told them what the Buddha had asked him, then he questioned them, "Is there some benefit in asking such questions?"

I do not observe this exchange from its worldly sense but from an entirely different standpoint. The Buddha came to this human world and taught us for forty-nine years and caused thousands of sutras to be written. But from our standpoint, this amounts to just one drop of rain. The conclusion of the Buddha's forty-nine-year sermon is just this: "Will it rain today?" or, "Nice day, isn't it?" Through these forty-nine years we have heard from the Buddha no more than the question, "How do you do?"

Nothing has changed in human life, and no evil has been conquered. Physically, perhaps, we have conquered epidemics, and we have conquered distance, but mentally we have conquered nothing. There is no beneficial deed that human beings have performed in these twenty-five hundred years since the Buddha taught us. From the Buddha's standpoint, he just told us something, and we gained nothing. So Buddhism brings no profit to human beings. Then why should we follow this teaching and promulgate it? Why should I sacrifice my own desire and that of my family and put on the Buddha's robe and speak about Buddhism? What is the benefit?

When Ananda asked the monks, "Is there some benefit in asking such questions?" the monks answered: "Asking about the condition of the weather, asking whether the alms-begging will be easy or hard today, we can think about the weather and about alms-begging 'intentionally.' By this attitude of thinking with a concentrated, intentional mind we can look up at the sky and carefully observe the movement of the clouds, or stretch out the palms of our hands into the air to feel the drizzling rain. We can stretch our bodies up onto our tiptoes to observe the faraway towns and the movement of the people in the streets, or we can decide what robes to wear, or whether it will rain or not, and which way to go, or give warning to the people following us. It is by transmitting to the people of the future world this knowledge of knowing something accurately that we can benefit them in attaining enlightenment. This is why we think the Buddha's asking us such insignificant questions brings great benefit upon us."

So there are two ways of coming to a conclusion on this question. When I think of these two conclusions, I think I gained nothing by studying Buddhism. But by my warning you that by studying Buddhism you will gain nothing, you will be brought to thinking accurately about what to do about following this Buddhist monk and listening to his Buddhist sermons.

The words which I have been using, however, this "gain nothing," I must explain to you, for their meaning is entirely different from the usual interpretation.

Ikkyu Zenji, one of the famous Zen masters of Daitokuji [38]—I belong to Daitokuji—said "What a rascal is he whose name is

Shakyamuni Buddha, coming to this world and bothering so many people!"

What was his point? We human beings were happy and simple, but because of the advent of Shakyamuni Buddha we became terribly worried and very busy. He bewildered us, and when we awoke to Reality, he gave us nothing. We found ourselves exactly where we were before.

Someone said Buddhism is like a toothache. When you are attracted by Buddhism, you go to the temple, listen to the monks lecture, give up your pleasure and time, buy books and bring them home, read them without sleeping, spend your life—ten, fifteen, twenty years—and in the end realize, "I was all right in the beginning; there was nothing to gain."

Well, the toothache is over, isn't it? When the tooth is aching, you run amok. But when the pain is removed, you just smile to yourself and say, "It's over."

I feel the same way. I went through terrific agony studying Zen. I lost everything I had, and I gained nothing. But this gained nothing is wonderful, and I am satisfied.

When Bodhidharma arrived in China from India, the Emperor Wu-Ti of the Liang dynasty [39] asked him a question: "I am building many temples, and I have made a law permitting men to become monks, and many people have been converted to Buddhism. Does my doing so bring any benefit?"

Bodhidharma answered, "No benefit. There is none."

We are still chewing this question as a koan, and many students study it.

So why did Bodhidharma say, "No benefit. There is none"?

Gaining benefit by doing something is an entirely human problem. If I am gaining something from Buddhism, I am not following Buddhism. This idea of benefit is such a small idea. Must there be something to gain from everything you do? Of course, today is a day of utilitarianism, we are utilitarianists. Every moment we are thinking about what we can get. To spend a whole life and in the end gain nothing? A wonderful conclusion to accept and make the basis of human life!

This gain nothing, the state of no-delusion, or no-filth, is attained by *anasrava*, which the Chinese translate as "no leakage," that which destroys filth or delusion, *klesha*, and purifies the mind. Desire is a filth. Delusion is a filth. Clinging to a conviction all of one's life is a filth. All of them are filth. When a human being rids his mind of filth, he attains the state of empty mind. The dead weight of mind is removed, and your insignificant mind-stuff is voided, and you become pure-minded, simple-minded. This doesn't mean you become stupid, however; it means you become wise. You can see everything clearly, for all mist is removed from your mind. The shimmering haze ceases, and you attain *samyag-dristhi*, the Buddha's "right view"—you see correctly according to the knowledge of Buddha. I sometimes think *samyag-dristhi* might better be translated as "legitimate view," but I am still thinking about it. When you look at something with a legitimate view, you don't look at it with like or dislike, emotion or delusion, or notion, but according to Law, the Dharma.

To gain nothing is always the conclusion of Buddhism.

# THE ROOT OF THE TREE

A s Buddhists, we have two directions toward which we are reaching: one is the attainment of enlightenment, the other is to render service to others. Attainment of enlightenment is the attainment of wisdom, *prajna*; to render service to others is to complete our love, *karuna*. Wisdom and love together are our aim. But wisdom is the Buddhist's faith, the foundation, and love is our aim. We educate ourselves to attain enlightenment; only then can we bring happiness to the world, to our home, and to ourselves. There can be no peace in the world, no happiness in the family, no quietude in one's self if one fails to attain one's own enlightenment. We must not fail ourselves. We must be true to ourselves. You can lie to someone else, but you cannot lie to yourself. If you lie to yourself, you have no life of your own. Buddhism teaches us to realize both of these aims. Enlightenment and rendering service to others is a twofold teaching.

Of the two great religions in the world, Christianity places its emphasis on love and Buddhism on wisdom, but they are not two different religions; they are one. If you were in a treetop and everyone else was in the topmost branches, all stretching out their hands to grip one another to make a unity, this would be the Christian approach to love. The Buddhist approach is different. We say we must first return to the root of the tree, to where all are embraced in a true unity in which individuality is lost. Of course, without branches there is no tree, and without the root there is also no tree. So we must have both. Christianity emphasizes associating in peace and unity, and loving one another. Buddhism teaches us to come back to the root and forget ourselves, where there are no numbers of people, but just one.

The ancients taught us that the world in which we are living is not the real world, but a temporary and mortal place. They taught us this in order to enable us to depart from it as monks or ascetics. Renouncing the world of turmoil, we take an aloof attitude and set our faces against it. This is the first step in entering religion. The next step is turning our face toward the world once again. We come back to the world and struggle along with everyone else and tell them about the real foundation of life.

Thus we have two attitudes in life. First we turn our backs to the world and face the truth. The direction of this attitude is from earth to heaven. In the second attitude, we face earth from heaven. This is the true attitude of the human being, and it is a great one. With it, we permit all the errors of human life, affirm everything on earth, and have sympathy with others in our compassion. But if we take the first attitude, looking from earth to heaven, and your friend happens to make an error, you will say, "Oh, I cannot associate with you!" The really great religious teachers never accuse others of their offenses. Men punish criminals, but great sages never have this idea, accusing their own brothers and sisters of their errors.

The second attitude, looking from heaven to earth, is the real attitude. However, to attain it you must first attain the real foundation of life, the enlightenment which is the attainment of wisdom. Then, and only then, can you turn to act with love toward others.

The foundation and the aim of life, then, are not two different things. Those who have no foundation for their lives have no aim either. We all have something upon which we can depend, have something for which we work, and which we worship. We live upon it as our foundation, and we render service to it.

The monks in China and Japan often talk about their faith when they meet a stranger. When a layman visits a monk, the monk usually asks him about his faith. You must always be aware of your faith. You must not live like a blind man.

# THE FOUR INVERTED VIEWS

There are many systems or contrivances that are used to enter Buddhism. If you want to climb Mount Shasta, Mount Rainier, or Mount Baker you must take a guide. The systems of Buddhism are also guides. Following them you can enter. Some think the terms used in Buddhism are Buddhism. This is like thinking a guide is the mountain. I hope you will not make such a mistake. If you think studying the terms of Buddhism is Buddhism itself, you are as foolish as thinking the mountain guide is the mountain, or looking at a menu and saying you enjoyed the dinner, even though you ate nothing.

The delusions of the ordinary man are said to be four, referred to as the Four Inverted Views (*viparyaya*). The Buddha said these inversions must be corrected. They are:

1) *nitya*: immutability, unchangeableness (as opposed to *anitya*, mutability, changeableness). Everyone tries to attain something that is unchangeable even though all is change.

2) *sukha*: ease, relief (as opposed to *duhkha*, agony). Everyone tries to find comfort while all is agony.

3) *shuddhi*: purity (as opposed to *ashuddhi*, impurity). Everyone tries to find purity in a world where no such quality exists.

4) *atman*: ego (as opposed to *anatman*, egolessness). Everyone believes in his own particular, separate soul, while all souls are united. The ordinary man cannot help struggling, and it is these four inversions that make it clear it is his thinking that causes the trouble.

The first inverted view is the wish that your father and mother might live forever; that you might keep your possessions forever; that you might live forever, while the fact is you are dying every moment.

All is transient. Even the earth is like a cloud in the sky; the mountains that were once the sea are now the desert. No one today believes the earth to be unchanging. We must realize this or we will suffer needlessly. Yes, today my face is smooth as velvet, and tomorrow it will be like brush, but I do not suffer because I know everything is transitory. Yet, as the Buddha said, "All sentient beings strive to attain eternity in mutability." Why? Life is agony—*duhkha*.

The second inverted view is to always try to find comfort. In summer we go to the state of Maine. In winter we go to Florida. We move back and forth all year long trying to make ourselves comfortable. Though our lives are busy, we are always frantically seeking tranquility. "Well, in my old age I will have time to become calm and to read all the philosophies." A long time ago I met the wife of the manager of the Hotel Astor here in New York. She showed me books of profound philosophy written in French and German. "As soon as I find time," she told me, "I'm going to read all these books." My friend, Mr. Miya [40], met her when she was sixty; she was still too busy to find a moment for study.

It is true that our world is busy and restless, and it is agony, and the Buddha said it very clearly. We know this, but we cannot decide whether it is really so. The struggle for existence is strictly a Western idea. When I was a child, I did not realize there was such a thing. When one is striving, of course, life is agony, because we have a body. There is scarcely a day something isn't wrong with mine. Today a headache, tomorrow a stomachache. Look at the world! Throughout history all cry, "Peace! Peace!" But there is no peace; human history is nothing but fighting. We had better accept it. Life is agony.

In this agony a man tries to find tranquility—"There is no rest in the city. I will go to the mountains." Once there, he runs to find a telephone so he can keep in contact with his business. One man went to a hot springs with a telephone in each hand! In Japan you can go to a mountain temple for a rest, but there at five-thirty in the morning all the monks begin to chant the sutras and strike the gongs.

It's not quiet at all! So you leave the temple and go to a cave, and there water drips, and you can't stand it. Where is quietude?

Once I went to the Mojave Desert. It was really quiet there, but it was so quiet I could hear my heart thumping. I was quite astonished at its noisiness. The idea that you can find quiet in some place is an inverted view. When you decide, "No matter how noisy it is, I will be tranquil. I will find tranquility here in the city," you soon become attached to the idea. But when the organ-grinder comes, you can't stand it, and you have to throw him money to go way. This kind of tranquility is just an idea. We also have the idea that mutability is *here* and eternity is *there*. Even in the last extremity, there is a struggle. "My soul is eternal," one cries. "There is no death." But he is still struggling with the idea when the great surge of death comes to wash him away from the surface of the earth.

We also add to our agony: "This is my last penny, and I am hungry, but I must hold on to it. Twenty years ago, I said I would keep this penny so I won't ever be penniless." When I came to America, my teacher gave me ten dollars in gold, saying, "This is for an emergency. Use it only at the last moment." I said, "Thank you very much," and used it when I first arrived. The last moment came very quickly! The Buddha did not condemn the ordinary man's inverted idea, but blamed his attitude towards it. When the time comes, one must drop the idea.

The third inverted view of the ordinary man concerns purity. Purity is also an idea. "All is impure and disgusting. I will go to the mountaintop, become a monk, and associate with no one." But there the monks are fighting, too, because they are jealous of one another. "I'll stay away from women. I won't even look at their faces," he vows. It is his mind that is impure. He does not understand real purity.

The fourth inverted view is the idea of a separate ego—"I must be president!" But to become president, he must struggle. A son says to his father, "Let me do it, Father." But the father replies, "No. I'll do it myself." The father must run the whole show by himself. The world is relative, but the ordinary man clings to his I-ness.

These are the four inverted views of the unenlightened person. There is another group of four inverted views held by *pratyeka-buddhas*. *Pratyeka-buddhas* are those who have attained enlightenment but still hold inverted views [41]. This is an important point. We call someone who has attained Reality "enlightened," but he may still hold the false view of mutability. Because of this, even though he has attained Reality, he lives in fear and dares not manifest himself in the world. When you pass the first koan, "Before father and mother, what were you?" you attain Reality. You realize nirvana, but you may still think that all is mutable and therefore valueless. If you realize that life is eternal, that this is Reality, why disvalue this life? The one who holds this view wants to stay in monotonous oneness forever because his enlightenment is not yet complete. In the koan, "When the candle flame is blown out, where does it go?" he answers, "Darkness is its own original aspect." This view is erroneous. Darkness! He thinks that monotonous oneness is the true aspect and that phenomena are the wrong aspect. This is the first inverted view of the *pratyeka-buddha*, who has no courage to affirm this phenomenal existence. If you stick to oneness, you think the Real does not exist in this world; you think Reality exists only in *that* world. This is not the true view. In the koan, "Stop the gong of the faraway temple," you take eternal silence as the Real and forget that the eternal gong from beginning to end is vibrating through the universe. Gong... oong... ong... ong.... ong... ong... ong...

You do not hear it, so you think that silence is the Real. When you observe another koan, "Stop the sailing boat on the faraway sea," you become still, thinking stillness is essential existence. That is your notion. The universal sailboat always moves, though you do not see this. When one attains true reality, one realizes that stillness is just an idea and so is a wrong view.

The second inverted view of the *pratyeka-buddha* is that you think you have to run away from agony. But if you really attain nirvana, really understand *dharmakaya*, where is the agony? The body aches. Where is the pain? In the last moment, in the pang of death, where is the agony? You cannot find it if you have really attained nirvana. And where is the purity flowing from that nirvana? Where are the impurities of this life? They are the waves of the natural current, of course. You must understand its law, then let your life flow with the current.

And fourth, in Buddhism, there is no ego. But when you attain nirvana, that is the ego—we say, this is not I, but Buddha. Of course, we do not mean Shakyamuni Buddha. Up to this point the enlightened one's attainment is only an idea, a theory. Now he must grasp that bunch of notions and throw them away; then he can really attain true nirvana.

From the Buddha's real view, both the ordinary and the holy man may have inverted views. If when you take *sanzen* [42], you answer from an inverted view, the teacher will never agree with your answer. The Buddha gave this teaching in order to destroy the human being's notions and to give him an idea of what Buddhism is.

To attain real nirvana, you must first destroy your false views. If you go to your teacher, sit there, and say, "There is nothing to say; there is no answer," this negative attitude is still an idea, still the holding of an hypothesis, so your teacher will never accept such an answer to a koan.

To enter nirvana is not so easy. To correct an inverted view is easy. But to throw away the ideas of immutability, tranquility, purity, and ego is difficult. And when you give up the second group of inverted views, as well, you will really attain.

# REAL EXISTENCE

B uddhism is one of the old religions with a doctrine that is very simple, can be explained plainly, and understood easily. To understand this religion, however, you must come into it through the front gate. Many scholars who have studied Buddhism have entered from strange corners. It seems to me they have never found the main entrance; they always come in through the chimney or the back gate, or the basement, or the window, never through the main entrance. They have lost themselves in the terms of Buddhism, which, of course, are very queer to them.

To explain that which was found by Shakyamuni Buddha two thousand five hundred years ago, it is customary to divide the main principle of Buddhism into two—that which relates to the outside and that which relates to the inside. The outside means the objective; the inside means the subjective. In my sect of Zen we do not have this division. From the first we grasp this principle without making an analysis of it. We just swallow it, or rather, enter into it. But in the Buddhism that must be explained by words, we must divide this one thing into two parts.

The observation of the ancients was simple. They observed the outside and thought it was a world consisting of four great elements: earth, water, fire, and air. In developed Buddhism, there is added the fifth element—ether [43]. In the Shingon sect of Buddhism [44], which you call the Mantrayana, the outside is divided into six elements, that is, earth, water, fire, air, ether, and consciousness—awareness, the power to know. Buddhists think awareness is entirely subjective; it cannot be objective. Men of the West also thought of the objective world as consisting of four elements. Perhaps in ancient times this was a universal view. Today, we divide the objective world into many elements and give many names to them, but this simple analysis can be of use as well.

Now we must talk about how to analyze the inside. I have already introduced to you many theories about how to analyze the inside, or mind. Today, you have your psychoanalysis, and we have our analysis of mind by meditation. Tonight, I shall speak of a theory which I have not previously introduced to you. This theory belongs to the Hosso sect [45], what the West has called the school of Buddhist psychology. Hosso (in Sanskrit, *dharmalakshana*) means the "appearances of *dharma*." In this case, *dharma* must be translated as "real entity." The things on my table are all appearances of real entities, as are the sky, the earth, man and animals—all are appearances of real existence. These appearances are temporary appearances; they are not real appearances. They are combustible, they can be annihilated, they can be destroyed—but the real entity that exists forever cannot be destroyed; it is eternal. Enlightened men can know the existence of the real entity directly, but ordinary human beings can only see temporary existences, so-called phenomena. The Hosso school explains phenomenal existence and points to Real Existence. The method of analysis I am going to introduce to you originated in India, but its terminology was developed in China. I shall not state the terms, but shall discuss the theory.

According to this theory, outer existence is of three natures: 1) the real circumstance, that is the real environment; 2) the circumstance of notion; and 3) that which is affected by notion, yet has its roots in Reality; it comes between the other two.

1) The nature of the real environment is different from the nature of plain environment. Plain environment is color, sound, smell, taste, touch, and so forth. Real environment is unintelligible to the unenlightened mind. The color red, for example. When I asked my mother, Why is red red? She said, Because it is red! Why is green green? Because it is green! Today mothers must explain to children that color is not in the object; it exists on the retina of the eye, just as sound is created on the drum of the ear. Color is the vibration of ether; sound

is the vibration of air. Your eardrum co-vibrates with the vibration of air and makes sound. So sound is not real entity. Something that is neither color, nor sound, nor taste, nor smell is real entity. In the West, this is called noumenon. You can't see it, but you know it exists.

As an entity, all New York is transparent. It has no color and no sound as you know it; it is created in your sense organs. We are living in an illusory world, not seeing the real world. But we must know and live in the Real world. When we observe this Real world with our five senses, it appears as color, sound, and so forth. But when we observe this Real world by our consciousness alone, without color, sound, without our five senses, then the whole world is just Real Existence, Real Entity. As Immanuel Kant called it, "Reality."

Though we know this is an illusory world, we cannot do anything about it. We cannot annihilate the color that comes into our eyes, we cannot refuse the sound that comes into our ears. We have to accept these as unavoidable existences. When we taste sugar, it is sweet; we cannot refuse the taste. When we drink water, it is tasteless, and we cannot do anything about it. But when you have water that tastes sweet, of course, this taste belongs to your tongue, not to the water; the water doesn't change, your taste changes. We must understand that such so-called outside things as color, and so forth, are isolated from our desire or emotion because they do not belong to the scope of will power. We say they belong to the scope of our consciousness. But this consciousness does not belong to us, it does not belong to the person. This consciousness is Nature's consciousness. When you think this way, you will change your view of the entire world.

When I went to Boston, a young man, a Mr. Robert Treat Paine Jr., asked me, "Do Easterners believe that the outside is not real existence?" I said, "Mr. Paine, we have nothing to do with it. Believe it or not, it is so, and logically, it must be so."

"Perhaps logically it's so," he said, "But we do not believe it; we do not accept it."

We both laughed, but I was a little surprised. We cannot accept it, but perhaps it is so. What can we do about it? The outside exists in our sense organs. This is the principal thing to us. Those of the Hosso sect say it is the nature of real environment.

2) Now we find the second circumstance that is entirely different from real environment in our mind—sheer notion. A notion is a plain and absolute existence within the human mind; it never existed outside; it was never introduced from the outside; and nothing is combined with it. It is plainly the production of the human mind, like the Ideal of Plato. He thought the Good, the True, and the Beautiful, was the Ideal. Every chair, for example, is an imperfect chair—nothing is perfect in the objective world, but behind this phenomenal chair is the Ideal chair that is perfect. Before that ideal chair all these temporary chairs must be ashamed! The Ideal, of course, is sheer notion. We can imagine many things that could never exist in the world. For instance, angels and such, which never have been and never will be existences. Notions have nothing to do with Reality, but they have their own position, their value in human life, and human beings are greatly affected by them. Without these notions, we could not create those things that give enjoyment to our intellect. However, notions are impressions or shadows in the mind, which have no real root on the outside and are entirely separated from any real circumstance.

3) The third kind of circumstance comes between the other two; it is that which is affected by our notions, yet has its roots in Reality. Dreams, for example.. There is no idea in a dream. We cannot control them; they take their own way. A dream is like a stream that flows by on its own way. I am trying to go somewhere in my dream and all of a sudden the street turns into a wood, and I am walking through the wood, and I come to a house, and it is my house. A succession of accidents happen in a dream. To a degree, we are controlled by these shadowlike notions, in the same way that we live in our emotional life. We can control the emotional, but we are always affected by it. It can be controlled, but not absolutely. We are always controlled by our emotions. The nature of emotion is like the nature of a dream.

When we meditate upon these three circumstances, or environments, we can see clearly how our mind is made up and of what it consists: the real outside that is related to our five senses and impressions of this outside that are concealed deeper in our consciousness that appear as dreams, daydreams, or thoughts. These thoughts and dreams are distilled, if I may use that word, and become notions. We meet a beautiful woman in the flesh, then we dream about her; then this impression is distilled some more and creates art—an angel, for instance. That is sheer notion.

As Buddhists, we must understand this notion as merely a notion. By this notion we cannot change or control real existence. Of course you will object: "But it is by sheer notion that we are changing our world! Franklin invented electricity, and with it we are smoothing off the tops of mountains and making the world a vegetable garden. Why do you say sheer notion cannot change the world? Why do you say it cannot change the outside?"

We say, perhaps you can take away a mountain, or wipe out the world by electricity, but you cannot destroy all the world, you cannot wipe out Reality, you cannot even change Reality. So we base our view of human life on this unchangeable reality. We observe all circumstances of human life and meditate on its many changes, upon the real material that we have stored in our minds during many incarnations. A queer word "incarnations," but our forefathers invented it, so we use it. Then we think, What shall we do about this matter?

Buddhists do not deduce anything from an idea—saying, "This must be so!"—first making categories and then trying to fit everything into them. In the past, your grandparents thought a woman's shape should be a certain way, something like a beetle's. So your grandmothers put on pads and corsets to walk out on the street. Notion created that shape, not Nature. An idea controlled it, not a woman's real shape. When you think about it, the morality we accept is also a notion, an idea into which we try to shape ourselves. The more this morality becomes stereotyped, the harder it is to adapt ourselves to it. Buddhists think differently. We try to adapt ourselves to unescapable Reality. We measure the inside of a square box with a square measure, and we try to make it accurate. We do not use a human measure to measure the outside. We make a measure to measure the outside: the idea cannot measure us. Whether the idea controls us, or we control the idea is a great problem to the human race. We have been struggling with it since we were born on this earth. We Buddhists think the moon is not always perfectly round. The reflection of the moon on the water changes its form a million times. Sometimes it is flecked with fish-scales, but a moment later it can be gathered to an amorphous state to suggest the perfection of the moon. We take the attitude of depending on Real Existence that is not notion.

# LEAKAGE AND NON-LEAKAGE

W hen you lose control of your mind, your notions flow out like dripping water. I find that American or Western people have noticed this flowing out of notions and have called it the "subconscious." Your conscious mind is the controlling aspect—how to speak, how to convey meaning—but your subconscious mind is not in your control. The subconscious is a term that comes from your schools of psychology, and it corresponds to our term *asrava*.

*Asrava* is a Sanskrit word meaning "to leak" or "to ooze," as you would perspire. This word was used in Buddhism from the Buddha's time to express the mind flowing out from our sense organs as water flows out from a broken tub. That which flows is *klesha*—your afflictions, the many vain thoughts and suffering notions that leak out from your mind like the pus discharged from a boil. *Klesha* are the leakages of desire and ignorance. The metaphor of leakage is not used in any other religious scriptures that I know of. *Asrava* and its allied term, *anasrava*, "non-leakage," are particularly Buddhistic, for these ideas are produced from the experience of meditation. Without the experience of meditation you will never apprehend the meaning of *asrava*, but when you practice meditation, you will immediately realize what it is.

Perhaps you have been to a Buddhist temple and have seen monks meditating surrounded by Buddhas. If you have and you want to go home and imitate their attitude, put your hands on your lap, straighten your back, stretch your neck, and breathe according to the rhythm of Nature. Hold your lower body on your crossed legs, and meditate upon your own mind. But do not meditate upon any word or notion. Do not meditate upon any symbol. Just meditate upon your own mind. If you are a beginner, I advise you to meditate upon all the sounds you hear. When you hear a piano, an elevator, an automobile, rustling paper, a palpitation of your heart—anything—meditate upon it, and not one by one, but all at once. Open your ear very wide and meditate upon sound until all sound comes and enters you. You are meditating upon the "outside," but all sound is produced from the "inside." Thus, you will naturally meditate upon your own mind. Then, after having meditated upon all sound, you will forget your mind, and you will forget you were concentrating on your audible sense, and then you will be aware of other things taking place, such as the leakage of notions—"Oh! I lent Mrs. So-and-So five dollars three years ago. I will telephone her, and tell her she must pay it back." One by one, your thoughts go round and round like a merry-go-round, and you are disturbed, and your face changes. If a teacher were watching you, he would shout at you, and then you would start again.

This is subconscious mind, *asrava*. In daylight you mostly forget it, but at night it comes out, and you dream it. When you have nothing to do in the afternoon, you daydream. When your strength of mind becomes feeble and loses control, it begins to leak. All year long you were healthy, but you felt there was some sickness in your body, though you thought it was under control. But now you are on vacation, and you are lying on the ground, and your body is limp, and all your energy has gone, and your mind is going around and around—going and coming, going and coming. But when your pocketbook gets empty, and you cannot stay any longer, and you buy your ticket and go back home to your office, this all stops. So when you understand what *asrava* is, you will naturally understand the state of *anasrava*. As I've said, *asrava* means "to stream," "to flow," so *anasrava* means "not to flow."

When pure objective existence is blended with your vain thoughts, you do not see its original aspect. If you overhear someone whispering, I'm sure you often take the meaning according to your own imagination. And because you like someone, you see her as a beauty, even though she's not. It's like the farmer who is very proud of his blend of fertilizer, thinking its odor is perfume. Or like someone who bakes a biscuit and thinks it very tender, when to you it's hard as stone.

It is with the knowledge of *nirodha*—cessation—that you attain pure *shila*, *samadhi*, and *prajna* [the commandments or precepts, meditation, and wisdom], the three basic principles of Buddhism. These principles annihilate all affliction. Therefore, *nirodha* is the cause of non-leakage and the state of nirvana. The attainment of nirvana is *anasrava*, no-leakage.

When the Buddha's disciples attain the stage of *arhat* [46], they have annihilated their worldly bodies and attained the Body of Reality. In Zen terms, they have attained *dharmakaya*, that which we practice in *sanzen*. The real meaning of *sanzen* is very pure. Sometimes students take *sanzen* carelessly. They blend their *sanzen* with their own emotions, their own sentiment, their own viewpoint. The true meaning of *sanzen* is the interviewing of the teacher in the state of *dharmakaya*. But in popular Mahayana, our physical body is the *dharmakaya* without knowing the real state of *dharmakaya*. So students take it for granted they can interview the teacher in the *sanzen* room with their worldly mind. The attitude of taking *sanzen* in *dharmakaya* is the same as the concentration of a cat watching a mouse—there is no room for the usual *klesha* in the mind.

When a disciple of the Buddha attains this state of *anasrava*, he realizes there is nothing he has to learn in this life. And when an *arhat* realizes there is nothing more to do, not a thing to do in this lifetime, he has attained arhatship, and has annihilated all afflictions, and he will never return to worldly life in future incarnations. He will stay forever in the state of Reality, which is the state of no-leakage. Therefore, no-leakage is a synonym for Reality as well.

In Buddhism there are six supernatural attainments. One of them is the knowledge of the annihilation of affliction. When we use our supernatural knowledge, people think it must be some miracle, or that there is something mystical about it, that one who has attained supernatural knowledge transfigures into a transparent body, penetrates stone walls and reaches the limit of the world. He walks on water, dives to the bottom of the sea, and walks through fire. To think like this is a sort of dilettantism. One who truly attains *dharmakaya* will never have these erroneous views. In *dharmakaya* practice, you realize that your upper body is the blue sky, and that your lower body is the black earth. You transfigure into the body of fire and the body of water. Those so-called miracles written about in the sutras are also practiced *by you* in *dharmakaya*. You prove it for yourself, and you never listen to the words of dilettantes.

In Buddhism the one who realizes his emancipation is aware that he has been emancipated and will attain the knowledge of how to emancipate others. Then he attains the dignity of an *arhat*. In the *Agama Sutras* [47] you can read these four lines:

*My life has come to an end.*
*My pure deed has been established.*
*My pure action has been performed.*
*I will not return again to this existence.*

This means my egoistic life of a heathen, my life of unbuddhistic behavior has come to an end. I have nothing to do with worldly affairs anymore, and I will not drink wine, handle money, steal, sleep with women, etc. All my worldly affairs have come to an end. Accordingly, my daily performance has come to an end. I will not return to the life suffused with afflictions. One who has become aware of this state has attained the state of the annihilation of all afflictions.

When all *klesha* are clearly wiped away and original darkness or ignorance (*avidya*) is destroyed, you will realize the state of *anasrava*. But when you are closing your eyes and you are still in darkness, covering your ears, and forgetting your own consciousness, you are hibernating in a mountain cave. If you are in that state, you are not yet in nirvana; you are still in the state of leakage. When the final state of meditation is completely destroyed, then you will come into the state of *anasrava*.

In the annihilation of afflictions there are two states:

1) All afflictions are annihilated by attainment, but ingrained habits are not yet cleansed [48]; attainment has only been the annihilation of afflictions. This is the state attained by the Zen students who have passed the koans "Mu [49]," "The Oak Tree in the Garden [50]," or "Sun Face Buddha, Moon Face Buddha [51]." The Zen student who has annihilated his afflictions with the power of these koans has only grasped the state that can be grasped through koans. But the ingrained habits, which have been acquired through many incarnations, are not yet annihilated. Therefore, his knowledge and his deeds are incompatible.

2) The second state is that of one who has annihilated leakage with his intellect as well as the ingrained or "perfumed" habits acquired through many incarnations.

The first is the state of the bodhisattva: the latter is the state of Buddha. Buddha annihilates his afflictions with his sword of wisdom, and is also emancipated from the long-permeating, acquired habits. The bodhisattva, with the sword of Manjushri, the bodhisattva of wisdom, has cut off all afflictions, but he remains in the bonds of permeating afflictions that he still bears in this incarnation.

There are many metaphors that explain this state of meditation. The mind must be empty to meditate upon Emptiness. The sky is empty, and you meditate upon the sky, but when the sky is destroyed, when you realize that there is neither sky, nor yourself, nor earth, you attain the state of *anasrava*. When you meditate upon a mirror, you look at the images reflected in it and realize that the reflections are not its nature. In *anasrava* you avoid all its images and become the mirror-by-itself, like a mirror standing in empty space with no reflections upon it. You think this is the state of *anasrava*, and you think it is the state of nirvana, but this mirror must be completely destroyed as well. Then you will realize the real state of *anasrava*. So the real state of *anasrava* is very difficult to attain.

# THE FIVE SKANDHAS

When you open the primitive sutras of Buddhism, you will find the five *skandhas* or "accumulations," from the first page. They are very important in Buddhism. The Buddha spoke about them from a very early period. These shadows of mind are like a sphere, a sphere that is the whole universe. If the sphere were made of light, there would be five shades of color, each enveloped in the other. According to Buddhism, our mind has five shades of consciousness: 1) *rupa*, appearance or form; 2) *vedana*, feeling or perception; 3) *samskara*, impulses; 4) *samjna*, conception; and 5) *vijnana*, consciousness. *Rupa* is material, physical existence, and *vedana* perceives it. *Samjna*, *samskara*, and *vijnana* are the inside world.

The first shadow, *rupa*, is on the surface of the sphere; it is the appearance of the physical and material body that is perceived by your eyes—your own body, the furniture about you, space, rivers, mountains, and oceans. They are your own body. They are as much your body as your flesh is your body, and when you look up at the sky, it is also your body.

The next shadow is *vedana*, it is feeling. This consciousness sees and hears and has the sense of smell, the sense of touch, and the sense of taste. It has the sense of feeling—to feel cold, to feel warm, to feel hot. This perception of outer existence can be compared to a box, and this outer existence is the lid. Without the sense organs we cannot see the outside, and without the outside, Nature would not bestow upon us the sense of hearing or seeing.

The third shadow is entirely different in nature. In a word, it is thoughts, *samjna*. When you close your eyes, you find them coming from the depths of your mind, and then you find them going. When one thought goes, another comes. Like a dream, they appear in your mind. You are in the dream, and your consciousness is perceiving them as your sense of sight sympathetically carries them. The relation between you in the dream and the consciousness which perceives them is very queer. Do you think you are perceiving yourself in the dream, or is it someone else who is perceiving you? You see your face, your body, yourself in your dream, but who is the one who is perceiving you? He who is perceiving you is not you yourself, it is consciousness. Whose consciousness is not generally talked about. Is it your consciousness or is it Nature's consciousness? We do not need to talk about it.

And then there is the fourth shadow, *samskara*. It is not very different from thoughts or dreams. In this fourth sphere everything is ephemeral, like a dewdrop that shines and then disappears, or like lightning in the sky. It flashes through your mind for a moment and then vanishes—you can hardly grasp it with your mind. *Samskara* are the "seeds" of thought, the seeds of emotion, the seeds of desire, the seeds of imagination. They are like feelings that cannot be put into words. What was that? How do I speak about it? You feel very queer. You feel something is disturbing you, but you do not know the reason, and then all of a sudden some person comes along and you shout out. A seed has entered your mind, and you clearly know what it is. Perhaps we can temporarily borrow the term "subconscious mind" for this.

*Samskara* is not only within yourself but in Nature, too. Though you cannot express it by words, you can come very close to it. Nature in this state of existence always has a powerful quality that asserts itself. When you are near a weeping willow, there is an element that conveys a sad feeling. The weeping willow speaks its own words to you. The pine tree also speaks its own words to you. A poet who wanted to speak about a pine tree would have to write ten or fifteen lines, but the pine tree speaks to you without a word. In such a way you feel that particular samskaric existence, as it speaks to your own *samskara*, your own feeling.

The fifth sphere is like the core of an apple. It is consciousness. As I said before, sense perception and outer existence are a box and a lid. The relationship between this sphere and that of *samskara* and *samjna* is also like a box. Consciousness is a box which has two lids, one lid which is made of fine material, *samskara*, and one which is made of coarse material, *samjna*, thoughts. As a whole our consciousness is not only "this" body, but everything. From the Buddhist standpoint, all outer existence is consciousness as well, so there is no matter at all. All is Consciousness. *Vijnana* corresponds to the color white.

When you meditate on these shadows of mind, you will reach the mother-consciousness, the *alaya-vijnana*, consciousness-itself [52]. Here you will find the one who meditates upon itself. You will also find that no one is meditating upon itself. It is consciousness-itself meditating upon its own mind. When you ask me if you need to meditate upon your own mind, I say no. Then what are you to meditate upon? Nothing. Here you will find the consciousness that is not yourself, but which to your deluded mind is ego, that which from your deluded state of mind you call ego. When you observe thus, your observation of the world, from the Buddhist standpoint, begins. So how do you observe these five accumulated shadows? When you find that they are nothing but shadows, you can then form the so-called Buddhist mind.

Now I am going to talk about this mind, how the Buddhist looks at the outside and how he looks at the inside, and how he abides in his own consciousness. Of course, the beginning of the Buddhist life is to puzzle about everything. No one can deny we have eyes, ears, a nose, a tongue, or a body that feels and a mind that perceives. These are the senses—the senses of sight, hearing, smell, etc. We have them, and without any theories we know we have them. Therefore, in Buddhism the senses are axiomatic. No one can doubt them. They are the foundation and the object of meditation. We meditate upon them as a substantial cushion upon which we can put our foot, something that doesn't shake, that can be the basic stone upon which to build our religion. This is particularly true in Zen. Zen is always desirous of finding that which is unshakable. It is very insubstantial when you sit to meditate upon a name such as "God" or "Buddha." It is like meditating upon a man made of snow. While you are meditating upon it, it disappears and melts away. You realize you have eyes and ears, and so forth, but don't pay attention to or put any value on these senses until you become blind or deaf. You pay them no respect. You don't know they are sacred. You use them as you use an old towel. You don't attach any special meaning to them. But if you meditate upon them, you will realize many things. If you are a true student of the Meditation School, they are the first thing you must meditate upon.

In Buddhism there are twelve entrances, *ayatanas*, of consciousness. Six are on the inside, the six senses (the six sense organs), and six are on the objective side, their objects (the six sense data or *dharmas*). The last one, number six, the mind (*manovijnana*), is really a combination of *manas* [53], the seventh consciousness and *dharma*. It is not existing outside, but between the outside and the inside.

Why do we call these entrances? Because consciousness enters them from inside to outside. Usually we think of entering a gate from outside to inside, but here, consciousness goes into these gates from inside and goes out to the outside. When you give water to a plant in a flower pot, water is absorbed from the earth and sucked up by the roots of the plant. The water enters the stem of the plant and then goes through and out the stems and leaves. Water enters from the inside to the outside. For you this way of observing is perhaps difficult, but for the Buddhist, it is natural.

So when we see this outside world, we meditate upon it. The tree is green... The flower is red... The sky is blue... Well, why is the sky blue? If you study optics, you will quickly find the answer. But the Buddhist will tell you color is not in the object but on the retina of your eye. It is a reaction and vibration in your eye. Then what is that which really exists outside? If color is here and sound is here, what is the entity that has been introduced as the vibration, the sound in my ear, the color in my eye, the pain in my body? Should I call the whole world "vibration"? "Power"? "Energy"?

The eye is a box, and color is the lid of this box. This is one unity, what I call *yoga* [54]. Ear and sound are another *yoga*; nose and smell, tongue and taste, body and feeling, mind and percept. Percepts are things which appear in your mind as shadows of the outside, but they are not entirely on the outside. They are in the *manas* region. Percepts are the seeds of concepts. Repeating the percepts many, many times we gradually form concepts. We pile concept upon concept and systematize them. Systematized conceptions we call knowledge.

The *alaya-vijnana*, not speaking here very carefully, is the subject of the percept. It became more important to Buddhist students later on. *Manas* is especially used in this case because it takes only the perceiving activity or part. Like a mirror, it only perceives and does not think. The nature of *manas* is such that it not only perceives, but also feels. It discriminates between beauty and ugliness, pain and pleasure. When its nature is to think or philosophize—perhaps the function of the brain—it is called *citta*. And *manas* that has no ability at all is simply the soul of an existing being, what we have called *hridaya*, the heart.

*Hridaya* is the soul of trees and weeds that we have within us. Our kidneys and so forth are like potatoes attached to roots, which are the intestines; the lungs are leaves, the heart flowers —there is a vegetable living inside the body of this human animal. This vegetable within our body is *hridaya*. It is different from your idea of "heart," which is the source of love, feeling, and emotion. Our idea of heart is the soul of a tree. If you want to know how a tree feels, you have it here.

The realization of this tree-mind is *samadhi*. You will hear many people say, "When I attained Zen, I was suddenly the tree standing there." Well, that is enlightenment for those people. Many times we come back to that area, but it is strange we realize it in the region of *citta*, the thinking mind. As human beings we cannot remove our thinking mind, so we have to do everything in it. Just as a baby cannot take milk without a bottle, or directly from the cow. Our thinking mind is this bottle, and the cow is *hridaya*. We cannot embody in the cow, but we can make the cow embody in us. So while I am in the region of *citta*, I can prove I am in the region of tree-mind, too. This *hridaya* region is intimately within us. When *citta* closes its eyes, we go back to the state of *hridaya*. While *hridaya* is working in the heart or the intestines, and so forth, our *citta* mind can take a rest.

So our mind is like a tower. There is the first floor, the second floor, and the third floor. *Hridaya* lives on the first floor, and *citta* on the second floor. Human beings are always living on the second floor. Mostly we are living in a deluded place, in the scum floating on the surface of *citta*. We must clean up that scum and live in pure *citta*. When you find *hridaya* and meditate upon it, and scrape away all queer notions and queer teachings and come back to clear, pure *citta*, and with this pure *citta* make direct contact with *hridaya*, that is Buddhism in its old form.

This is merely an outline, but it is a very important subject for Zen students. It is one on which you should meditate. The Zen student should know what he sits upon. Pay respect to your mind. Worship it day and night. It makes a religion, you know.

There was once a monk who put a candle in a dark room every night, and offered flowers and incense. A novice questioned him about it, "Why do you offer flowers and incense when there is no image?"

The monk said, "I offer them to my eyes, for I worship my own eyes."

# THE PRACTICE OF RUPA SKANDHA

The five shadows or *skandhas* of consciousness are the funda-mental delusion of sentient beings. Destroying these shadows one enters pure nirvana. So they are the backbone of the Buddhist system. Without them there is no Buddhism, as all other principles are derived from them.

To find pure *rupa* is the first practice of a Buddhist. To find pure physical appearance, to find pure phenomena relating to our two eyes is the first practice. We think we are looking at something. We think we are observing something. We think we are observing the outer world. If you look into your mind, you will find that you are not observing outer existence but that you are observing your own notion, your own idea. When Japanese come to this country and begin to study English, their teachers say, "Up!" so the Japanese say, "Up!" Their teachers say, "Perfect!" so the Japanese say "Perfect!" The Japanese think they are listening to the teacher's pronunciation, but they are not, they are listening to their own mind. It is the same when you begin to study painting, you imitate the blue after the sky. You think blue sky, so you get a tube of blue paint and paint your blue sky with it. When you bring it to your teacher, he says, "What is this?" You say, "A blue sky, sir." But the teacher says, "Are you mak-ing a catalogue of paints, or are you making a painting?"

Our eye is a very poor eye. Deluded by our thoughts, we cannot see the real outside. To see the real outside is the first practice of Buddhism—we avoid our notions and our own preconceived ideas. We try to look at the outside, not with our minds, but with our eyes. We do not try to be artists, but try to avoid notions, our conceived mind-stuff. Then we try to correct our feelings or perceptions (*vedana*), our thoughts (*samjna*), and then our impulses (*samskara*).

*Samskara* is not thought; there are no thoughts in it. It is like emotion, deeper than thoughts; it is more like mood. So we try to correct the distortion in our emotions. Then there is consciousness (*vijnana*), or sometimes, conscience. You say "good" conscience, "bad" conscience, but the Buddhist's conscience is neither good nor bad. If you try to use a good measure to measure the world, then the world is bad. If you try to use a bad measure to measure the world, then the world is good. Usually man tries to measure the world with a homemade measure—that is, his own measure, not an authentic measure—and to judge this as good and that as not good with it. He thinks his good is always correct, and the whole world always wrong. We must destroy such homemade measures and get a universal measure not made by man.

These five practices are nothing but the practice of the Buddhist, but first you must know, must understand, what *rupa* is; what physical, material appearance is. If you do not know what the physical world is, what material appearance is, you cannot free yourself from avarice, the inordinate desire for gain—you get one, you want to get two; you get two, you want to get four, and five, six, seven, eight, one hundred, two hundred, four hundred! There is no end to it. Avarice is the most painful torture when it cannot be satisfied [55]. But when you understand what *rupa* is, you will give away your avarice and free yourself from it; you will not be a mass of avarice anymore. This is the Buddha's teaching.

When the Buddha said you must understand what *rupa* is, what phenomenal appearance is, he was talking about what THIS is—we know that One Thing exists. Temporarily, we call it Reality. Really, we do not know by what name to call it, but a name is not necessary. In Zen study, when you enter the Zen room and pass the first koan, you will get into this Reality.

In Buddhism we call Reality *dharmakaya*. Reality cannot be described by words. There is just one. We do not need to call it "one" but when we use words, we have to call it something. When you get to Reality, there is no word to utter, no way to think about it. Reason cannot enter there, but fortunately we have intuition. There is no way to reach Reality but through the avenue of intuition. Intuition is wisdom that is without the experience of the eye, the ear, or reason. You immediately realize what this is when I strike my gong. But do not make any mistake in perceiving this Reality. When you say "Reality is…," you are only reasoning about it, thinking about it—you have not realized it. It is reason, not Reality. Reason will not take you into Reality. Your eye will not take you into Reality. When you try to get into Reality, get your brain and throw it out, and throw aside your physical body as well. There is just one avenue and one hope, and that is through intuition. Through intuition you immediately prove Reality. Reality is not a dream. Reality is not a faraway country. Reality is not heaven. It is here, everywhere! This is Reality.

When you understand Reality through *rupa*, then you must enter deeper and realize it through your perceptions, then through your thoughts, and so on, until you enter nirvana. Through nirvana you get into Reality. This is Buddhism. Through all the sutras the Buddha speaks of nothing but Reality.

Truth is everywhere: in the gutter, on the streetcorner. But you must observe it with your own true experience. When the Buddha said, "Take clay and make gold," he said you must get truth from the gutter and the streetcorner, and experience it through your wisdom. Then you will understand.

There was a fisherman in China who for forty years used a straight needle to fish with. When someone asked him, "Why don't you use a bent hook?" The fisherman replied, "You can catch ordinary fish with a bent hook, but I will catch a great fish with my straight needle."

Word of this came to the ear of the Emperor, so he went to see this fool of a fisherman for himself. The Emperor asked the fisherman, "What are you fishing for?"

The fisherman said, "I am fishing for you, Emperor!"

If you have no experience in fishing with the straight needle, you cannot understand this story. Simply, I am holding my arms on my breast. Like that fisherman with the straight needle, I fish for you good fishes. I do not circulate letters. I do not advertise. I do not ask you to come. I do not ask you to stay. I do not entertain you. You come, and I am living my own life.

If you fish with the straight needle, life is easy, and there is no danger of your hooking yourself. When you get the truth and let it pass through your wisdom, then you have true religion. With one koan you will understand the law of the universe, and you can acknowledge the truth in each stage of the life of all sentient beings. All experiences go through your true wisdom, which is the wisdom of Reality. If you understand *rupa*—if you understand what *rupa* is in the original sense—you will emancipate yourself from all avarice.

# THE BUDDHA'S SKANDHAS

There is nothing to be compared with Buddha's *skandhas*. His *skandhas* are those of one who is beyond all things. His *skandhas* are those of superlative enlightenment. For Buddha's enlightened mind is without leakage. The usual *skandhas* are those of a leaking mind, but Buddha's *skandhas* are of a non-leaking mind. Everyone's mind is like water that is leaking out of a broken tub. When you meditate a little while, you see, you feel, you realize that many things are leaking out of your mind. Buddha's mind, however, is in the state of no-leakage, the state of nirvana.

The Chinese translated "Buddha's *skandhas*" as "the five divisions of the body of Dharma." The body of Buddha is constituted of these five parts of mind-essence. In Hinayana Buddhism they are the Buddha's *dharmakaya*. They are like five branches that are connected into one *dharmakaya* root. In Mahayana Buddhism, however, the *dharmakaya* is the body beyond Buddha himself—it has no parts. In Hinayana Buddhism, Buddha's living body itself is *dharmakaya*, which comprises five parts: 1) *shila*, 2) *samadhi*, 3) *prajna*, 4) *vimukti*, 5) *vimukti-jnana-darshana*.

1) *Shila* means precepts, the commandments. Human beings have this compass innately in their minds, like the compass on a ship that always points to the North. You drink wine, but if you drink too much you put your hand to your head and say, "Why have I drunk so much!" Your compass is keeping the balance.

Buddha's *shila* is detached from all the offenses that the usual human being commits. Buddha's every act, the karma that is created by his body, by his mouth, by his mind, all are entirely free from any of the offenses that are committed by human beings. Buddha attained the essential body that possesses the virtue of commandment. The commandments that Buddha observes are not commandments imposed upon him by someone else, as are the commandments that the monk observes. The monk observes commandments given to him by his teacher—you shall not kill, steal, lie, commit adultery, etc. The monk observes these rules, but for Buddha the observation of commandment is simply a spontaneous, instinctive act. Whatever he does he always acts in accordance with *shila*. Buddha's essential body of commandment is *dharmakaya*. Buddha's *dharmakaya* has this virtue, innately. When we observe and study commandments, we realize all of a sudden that this is the essential body of commandment. So we do not need all those rule books. We can throw them in the fire, for all essential law is written in our hearts. The pigeon returns to its own nest, though it is not educated to do this; it is its natural orientation. So we, from bewildered, conscious acts, return to the instinctive observation of commandments. This is our homing instinct.

The baby chick knocks on the inside of the shell to let its mother know that it is ready to come out. At almost the same moment the mother hen pecks at the outside of the shell and the shell is cracked so the little chick can emerge. A Zen master has this same instinct. When a pupil comes to that point, the master takes hold of him and pulls him out. Sometimes, however, the master must push the pupil back again into the shell. A mother chicken cannot do this to the baby chick. A Zen master can pull the trigger twice, but even he cannot pull it a third time!

2) *Samadhi* is the Buddha's original mind; it is beyond all afflictions and sufferings; it is calm and tranquil. Buddha's original mind instinctively possesses *samadhi* and tranquility. The Buddha observes that the world is in agony but that no one in the world has an ego. No one suffers. Therefore, suffering essentially belongs to a deluded mind. When you free yourself from your ego and from the residence of your ego, you will attain the *samadhi* of emptiness.

When you attain emptiness, you attain the state of no-form. Everything has a form as a man, a woman, an animal, an insect, but you are freed from all limited forms—all objective existences. Then you reach the state of annihilation (*nirodha*). The state of annihilation is the state of nirvana. You realize that all your desires and hopes are quenched. All sentient beings are converted into this nirvana. You realize that there is no Buddhism to be promulgated and that there are no sentient beings to be saved. You relinquish three things—ego, form, and purpose. Thus you return to your own tranquility, your own *samadhi*.

3) *Prajna* is the Buddha's attainment of perfect wisdom, the original nature of Dharma, that is, *dharmata*. When we observe the koan, "Before father and mother, what is your original aspect?" its destruction will bring the attainment of that perfect wisdom that is the innate nature of the whole universe. The koan is not a thing that you are to think about; it is a thing to be destroyed. When you have the power of wisdom, the koan bothers you. The koan saturates your mind, stains the color of your mind, tarnishes your mind. Use the strength of your mind to destroy the koan. The koan is a touchstone to test whether your wisdom is pure gold or not. *Prajna* is, therefore, the original wisdom of Buddha. It is like the light of a lamp. I do not add light to the lamp; it is the electricity that has light, and that can destroy that which is combustible. So Buddha's *prajna* is also like fire. With his power he burns the koan and reduces it to ashes. Thus he solves all the questions of sentient beings; it is his instinct. When he destroys all the questions of sentient beings, he is free from all the bonds of affliction, free from all the bonds of suffering and doubt. Thus he attains emancipation, *vimukti*.

4) *Vimukti* is the attainment of not residing in form, neither in color, nor sound, nor mind-stuff—the state of nirvana, that which embodies all virtue and potential power. If you attain the state of nirvana you do not die. You feel that you have really touched a magnetic center. It gives you strength. When you are weak, you are all entangled. When you become strong through many years of training, as Buddha trained himself under the *bodhi* tree [56], you destroy all traps and snares; you leave them behind, you attain emancipation.

5) *Vimukti-jnana-darshana* [57] is when you know you have attained entire emancipation; you are aware of your attainment. Without this awareness you cannot say that you have been emancipated or enlightened. This is something that you can really grasp, though grasp is not a very good word. It is better to say this is something that you can embody yourself in, as I am embodied in this body and know that I am here. A charlatan cannot do this. Without this awareness you cannot teach anything to another.

This awareness of emancipation is called in Buddhism "the wisdom that is attained subsequently." When you just pass your first koan, you enter the universe of *dharmakaya* without clear awareness. You stand in the middle of *dharmakaya* like a newly hatched chick, or like a newly born infant. Then, day by day you gather this awareness. Your awareness goes into all the details, all the branches of sentient life, as a baby grows up day by day and gains his awareness of his mother, his father, the taste of milk, of food, etc. You must have this awareness in the world of *dharmakaya*. A human being must have awareness of his emancipation, awareness of the wisdom of complete emancipation.

When you attain the essential body of commandment you realize the form of commandments. You are like a fire that burns the whole field, like water that covers the entire field, or like a wind that sweeps everything away. The form of commandment usually stands on the *sambhogakaya* standpoint. With this power of commandment you can destroy everything. Then you will come into the written commandment, the *nirmanakaya* view.

By observing the commandments, you will gain tranquility in every place. By this tranquility you will attain wisdom. By this wisdom you will attain awareness of emancipation. One who attains Buddha's *skandhas* will be supported by the lower sentient beings, by *devas, nagas, yakshas, gandharvas, garudas, kinmaras, magoragas* and *kumbandhus* [58].

# EMANCIPATION

Buddhism is a religion of self-realization. It is not a religion that can be taught. In Buddhism, you must realize the experience of Buddhism entirely by yourself. A Buddhist monk, therefore, is not a teacher. He does not teach anything. He does not teach his attainment to others. He just pursues his own attainment, and those who are sympathetic with his attainment follow him. When I first came to this country, I was asked about this attitude — "What is your activity in Buddhism?"

I would say, "Sitting and meditating."

"Meditating upon what?"

"Upon nothing."

"Nothing? Your religion has no charity? You just meditate? Do you call that religion?"

"Yes."

Of course, they are dumbfounded, because the Buddhist idea of attainment is to pour water into a glass, and when it fills up, it runs over. Before it is filled, however, we must fill it. So we do not have time to give anything to people.

A Buddhist monk works for his own emancipation. When famine attacks the country, he sits by the roadside and joins his hands waiting for his last moment. When he is sick, he closes his eyes and without tears, without pangs of death, dies alone. When he hasn't a penny, he stands with his bowl in his hands under the eaves of a layman's house, not asking and not begging. If no one gives him anything, he joins his hands and starves to death. When he comes to a foreign country, no one knows him, no one follows him. He scrapes the floor, he licks the dust, he supports himself. This is the Buddhist monk.

Emancipation means that you disengage yourself from all the bonds that fasten or rope you, visible or invisible. The ropes of karma and affinity are binding you and taking away all freedom from you. But by your own endeavor, you unfasten these ropes and free yourself from bondage of all kinds. The things that are fastening you and taking your freedom from you are your karma, the results of your previous deeds—as your father was a drunkard, therefore you, as your father's child, have some mental affect. It bothers you all your life, and you act queerly. You call it "inheritance." We call it karma. When you were young perhaps you associated with a Buddhist monk, so when you graduate from your Christian seminary you still carry a little inclination towards Buddhism in your mind. There is, of course, both good and bad karma, and both take freedom from you. When you unbind these invisible ropes by your own effort, you attain freedom of mind, and you emancipate yourself from the agony of worldly life. It is said in the *Mahaparinirvana-sutra* [59]: "To attain nirvana is *moksha*." This is a very big word. To attain nirvana means to transcend this phenomenal world, to experience the state of Reality. This is the meaning of *moksha*.

There are several kinds of nirvana. The layman thinks after death he will enter nirvana—unless he goes to hell. This is negative emancipation. Positive emancipation is *vimoksha*—by your own enlightened mind attained by experiencing the state of nirvana, you emancipate yourself from this world, but remain in it. Suppose your house is infested with cockroaches. If you try to get free from them by moving out, or you set fire to the house, that is the negative way—as you think to attain nirvana by annihilating the phenomenal world. The other way is to ask an exterminator to come and kill the cockroaches without destroying the house. That is the positive way. Meditating upon your trouble, not running away from it, but remaining in it, you can find the solution to what to do. You must find emancipation from your worldly attachments, from your greed, from your selfish love or desire. You must emancipate yourself from your ignorant mind, from deluded emotion, and from all superstition.

Wisdom, of course, is the cause of both kinds of emancipation. Without our minds, we could not emancipate ourselves from emotion or scientific delusion because it is our wisdom that emancipates us. We can attain nirvana with the intellect by meditation, but we will be "caught" in meditation. This is a very important point in the doctrine of Buddhism. When in meditation we have annihilated the outside in the attainment of nirvana, we are still, nevertheless, in meditation; therefore, we must annihilate the state of meditation, of *samadhi*, as well in order to attain the next stage, absolute annihilation.

So, there are *arhats* who have attained nirvana by intellectual power, and those who have not attached to intellectual power, but have hopped out from everything and attained absolute freedom. There are those who have experienced *moksha*, and others who have experienced both *moksha* and *vimoksha*. And there are yet those who have attained what is called *pratimoksha* [60]—Buddha's *skandhas*. While those who are deluded have the usual *skandhas*, those who has attained absolute freedom have enlightened aggregations. With the Buddha's *skandhas*, we act according to the Buddha's commandments, and following these commandments—*pratimoksha*—we emancipate ourselves at every moment. One by one, we emancipate ourselves with our enlightened mind.

When we attain freedom from the five shadows, we emancipate ourselves from the physical body. How do I emancipate myself from this physical body, this *rupa*? I meditate upon the physical body, upon the fact that it is existing from beginningless beginning to endless end; that it is not my body. As I see my body existing, it is my illusion, and I know its true realization, etc. Thus I emancipate myself from *rupa*. Thus I also emancipate myself from perception—*vedana*. I emancipate myself from conception—*samjna*. What is my mind? What is this dream? I emancipate myself from mood—*samskara*. This consciousness—*vijnana*. I meditate upon *vijnana*, and I emancipate myself from consciousness.

This is *pratimoksha*.

# THE PRACTICE OF NIRODHA

Ananda once asked the Buddha: "What is *nirodha?*" The Buddha replied, "*Nirodha* is the annihilation of *rupa. Rupa* has nothing to do. *Rupa* is created by relation. Therefore, with no desire, with no purpose, you attain the annihilation of the body."

The Buddha's explanation was very clear, but it is contrary to the usual notion of annihilation. When the Buddha said "body," he meant the body of the whole universe. We Buddhists do not make a distinction between the human body and the substance composing all other bodies in the universe. All return to the four great elements. The sky is my body. The earth is my feet. Water is my blood, and air my breath. Why should we make imaginary lines between this and that? Is the human body more important than the entire universe? This entire body has nothing to do. It is purposelessness. It exists when this is created, and when this is destroyed.

The practice of *nirodha* begins by annihilating the *skandha* of appearance, then of perception, conception, impulse, and consciousness. When we annihilate the soul function of consciousness, we find the Law ends. We also see bottomless nirvana, which is Tathagata, the true Buddha. But if you try to see this Buddha with your consciousness, you cannot. You must annihilate your consciousness to realize nirvana. But this does not mean you should leap from a cliff, thinking to enter nirvana by annihilating your physical body. Such a Buddhism is poison. You must avoid this kind of misunderstanding. This was the reason Ananda asked the Buddha about the meaning of *nirodha.*

Buddhism is not a good friend of the theory of evolution, nor is it a bad friend. As long as human beings exist, the sense of a purposeful universe will grow sharper. But, after all, everything is created by the relation of the elements in purposeless work. If you observe this without desire or purpose, you will annihilate the body. Do you understand this conclusion? It is an important point in Buddhism. Phenomenal existence has nothing to do with you, or you with it.

When I observe man, without desire or purpose, I annihilate him [61]. But then, of course, you say, "But this phenomenal existence does not disappear!" No, annihilation has nothing to do with appearance or disappearance. It is not necessary to suppress desire or purpose, but you must have nothing to do with the universe at this moment—no desire or purpose relating to it. You need not destroy the body, the five senses, or phenomenal existence, but you *must* annihilate it. This is the knack in understanding the Buddha's Buddhism.

Then you must annihilate perception. How do you do it? If when you try to annihilate pain, try to stop pain, you say you have nothing to do with it, you annihilate it. It is not easy. If you have any idea that connects you to the pain, you will not annihilate it. This difficult practice is the way to enter nirvana. But if you say, "There is no sin; therefore, I can commit any crime," you have fallen into a dangerous pit.

And when you annihilate consciousness, you have nothing to do, you have no desire and no purpose. To your eye, the flower is red; to your body, silk is smooth; to your mind come thoughts of flowers and of silk. Your consciousness reflects this. But *you* have nothing to do with it. The deep sea of nirvana is peeping out. This is *nirodha* and the gate of Buddhism. Funny gate!

I do not want to push anyone from the corner of a cliff. Without purpose or desire, you must come to the cliff and see the bottom. What do you see? *Nirodha*. Once you realize *nirodha*, you have really found your foundation of soul. Then you will turn out once again—from consciousness to impulse, from impulse to conception, from conception to perception, from perception to appearance.

Now, in all emotion, desire, and purpose, you are the one who knows Buddhism, which is religion.

The road is straight, and you are free from all entanglements.

# THE ONE THING

O ne day, while the Buddha was sojourning in Jeta's Garden [62], he addressed the following words to his disciples:

*Bhikshus* [monks], *you must regard one thing always. To regard this one thing, you must clear away the five afflictions regarding this one thing, and you will attain the four grounds.*

When you examine your own efforts toward attainment, you will usually discover two kinds of debility. One of these occurs in meditation when your mind is out of control; it is leaking. Perhaps, as a beginner, you use a *mantra* [63] when you are meditating. While you are repeating this *mantra*, something comes up to distract you, all kinds of thoughts stray through your mind, as water leaks from a wooden vessel. This happens because your mind is not yet concentrated, not yet essentialized, not quite crystallized into the absolute, essential mind. Your mind oozes mud like a sieve, and you keep much impure matter there. You must drive all this unnecessary mind-matter out of the essential part of the mind that is the center of awareness. And if you do not repeat a *mantra*, you may have even less control, and the mind may carry you away. Finally, however, you will find the essential mind, and from that center no mind-ooze will leak forth.

The other debility has to do with actions, doing. If in your actions you and Nature make complete contact [*yoga*], so that you cannot draw any distinction between yourself and Nature, you are not doing anything. For example, when a farmer sows his seed in the ground in early spring it grows, but the farmer is not doing anything. Getting up in the morning and going to bed at night you are not doing anything. But when you are sleepy and you try to keep awake by taking strong coffee, you are doing something. When you are hungry, you eat. But if you eat when you are not hungry, you are doing something. When you do something—in this sense of the word—you are not entirely a Buddhist, for from this kind of doing there are always bad results. You are a true Buddhist only when you are not doing anything.

The "one thing" the sutra tells you to regard is the main principle of Buddhism. From morning to evening you must regard this one thing. As you regard this one thing you must always bear in mind whether there is leakage or no-leakage, and doing or no-doing. When you use your mind you must ask yourself: Is this a vital function of Nature, or am I doing it? Carefully observing from these two double points of view, you will reach the gate of nirvana, and from the gate of nirvana you will arrive at understanding. As you look into the sky, suddenly you will see the dark gap of the heavens revealed before you. Thus observing the leaking or non-leaking of the mind, and the artificiality or naturalness of your actions, you do not need to read anything, or practice anything. It is essential only to regard the one thing, from morning to evening. All commandments are founded upon doing-non-doing; all meditation is founded upon leakage-non-leakage. There is no other Buddhism.

To arrive at this point, however, you must first clear away the five afflictions.

The first affliction is your body-view. You think your body exists separately, apart from the rest of the world. But it exists only because the four great elements exist. The air will dissolve the flesh, and the bones will turn to powder. As a separate thing, this body does not exist, and neither do the five aggregates of mind. But because you believe that your body separately exists, you feel that it belongs to *you*, and so you have the idea of possession.

The second affliction originates in the first. Because you think your body exists separately, you believe that after death the form of your body will continue to exist. You make pictures of heaven and hell and you are there in human shape. You have an image of yourself you call your astral self, perhaps possessing eyes, ears, and hands. Either this, or you go to the opposite extreme and say that there is nothing after death—no energy, no thought, no vibration, no record of the deeds of this life, all is wiped out.

The third affliction is thinking there is no system of causality in this life or after death, and that there is no corresponding result for one's actions; doing good, you may expect bad results; doing evil, you may expect to be rewarded.

These three are not such terrible afflictions, there is still hope. But the fourth and the fifth afflictions leave none.

The fourth is never thinking for oneself, but always taking someone else's thoughts to act upon.

The fifth is clinging to a literal interpretation of the commandments. The monks of ancient India were required, for example, to dwell out-of-doors under trees. Now, India is a warm country and the commandment can be observed literally there, but how would you keep this commandment if you lived in Alaska? Therefore, you cannot follow such commandments literally. You must look for the principle behind each of them, and apply it accordingly. You must find your own commandments.

These afflictions, then, must be cleared up, and when they have been eliminated by regarding the one thing, you will find the four grounds.

The first ground is desire, the desire to enter *samadhi*. (One is always exhorted to annihilate desire.) This desire will bring you to *samadhi*. You work hard all day, then you go to bed and examine your mind to see whether or not it leaks. If it is leaking, you must ask yourself why. Only actual practice by the mind can bring you to *samadhi*, and it is desire that will lead you to make that effort.

So, the first ground is desire; the second is *samadhi*; the third is *dhyana* [64]; and from *dhyana* you will arrive at the fourth, observation.

For any sentient being these teachings are enough for one lifetime.

# THE TWO KINDS OF ANATMAN

A *tman* is something that is considered the "supervisor" of oneself. It is like the king, president, master, or boss of a concern. Human beings believe they have such supervisors within themselves. Almost all religions in the world have a god who is the supervisor, and the one who attaches to the view that one has a supervising soul within, called "ego" in human beings. But the Buddha believed there is no ego in either man or *dharmas*—here *dharmas* means that which is in Nature [65]. There is no ego in anything. There is no ego in man, and there is no ego in *dharma*. Therefore, these non-egos are called in Sanskrit, *pudgala-dharma-nairatmya*. This term is used in the *Lankavatara Sutra* [66].

So there are many types of attachment to ego. The *Diamond Sutra* [67] says there are four kinds of belief in ego, and that those who believe in these four *atmans* do not attain *prajnaparamita*. The four kinds of ego are: 1) the ego within the human being; 2) the ego within mankind; 3) the ego within sentient beings; 4) the ego within long-lived beings.

Even if you deny ego in yourself, you believe there is something supervising all mankind. Perhaps there is no soul in animals, or other sentient beings, but there must certainly be a soul in human beings. Or you think that not only mankind has a soul, but there is a soul in all sentient beings. That there is *atman* in the long-lived being means that there is some soul like a god that lives forever and never dies— Atman. Some half-baked Buddhists believe that it is the *alaya*-consciousness that is the long-lived being. It is clear in the *Lankavatara Sutra* that the *alaya*-consciousness is not final, is not final being, just as the human body is the aggregation of the five *skandhas*, and the five *skandhas* are temporary. So there is no supervisor within us.

There is no *atman* in our eye, no *atman* in our ear, no *atman* in our perceptions, no *atman* in our reasoning, and no *atman* in our moods, and no *atman* in our consciousness. If there is no outside, there can be no inside that is called consciousness. Outside and inside are relative existences, neither of which is the supervisor.

Some think there is no soul within man, but that the soul is outside of man, in the same way that there is no fire in the furnace, but fire can be brought into the furnace from the outside, and then makes a flame. Some chemists take such a view. Life did not exist in the human being of itself, but came from another planet or star to this star. High heat produces the soul, but human beings have no means of creating high heat, so we cannot create life—the ego is outside.

But the Buddha taught us that all outside is relative existence. If there were no fire, there would be no water, no earth, and if there were no earth, there would be no water, no fire. All are existing relatively. If one appears, all appear; if one disappears, all disappear. Therefore, outside has no ego. It is like a stream of water in a river; the water in the river has no ego.

It is also like the seed of a plant. When spring comes, the seed sprouts; when summer comes, it blooms; when autumn comes, it dries; when winter comes, the seed matures and drops to the ground. It is all relative, so there is no ego in it.

It is also like a candle flame, or like the wind. The wind blows from the east, from the west, from the south, from the north, but there is no ego in it.

Or, like the circling dippers fastened to a wheel in Japanese wells. When the farmer walks on the wheel, the dippers pour water onto the field. Each dipper carries water, but there is no ego within each dipper.

Therefore, there is no ego in life, or in death, and there no ego in the transmigrations of sentient beings either. Transmigration is like the magic created by a magician. When the magician uses a little cloth and makes a fish or a horse that jumps around, or uses his hand to produce fire from his palm, it's all an illusion. All this phenomenal existence is illusion—there is no ego in the illusion, and there is no ego either inside or outside.

Those who observe no ego within man are the Hinayana students. In this way they annihilate their sufferings and attain nirvana. To those in the Hinayana, I have no ego. My suffering is not my suffering; there is nothing that suffers. Like one who is standing in a storm, the storm is not mine. My soul is immobile. This is how he thinks. So when he is sick and in pain, he suffers, and he is ill, but "he" is nobody. He accepts suffering only. He accepts all suffering bravely and without complaint. With his natural and empty mind, he observes sickness, and he cures sickness. It is the virtue of the non-ego view. But it is Hinayanistic.

When I observe all of this outside, there is no ego—the chair has no ego, the table has no ego. In Greek Idealism, the chair has its own "ideal" chair. All the chairs that appear are imperfect, but behind all phenomenal chairs there is the perfect idea of the chair. All chairs are ashamed of their present condition. But through time, all chairs will gradually attain the state of perfect chair.

As Buddhists, we must laugh at this conception. All takes shape in Nature according to circumstances, that is, relation, as the moon is reflected in water. In accordance with the movement of the water, the moon takes all kinds of shapes. The moon doesn't assert itself in the water, saying it must always be round. Though the moon's reflection be in one thousand pieces, there is perfection within. That is the non-ego attitude.

So if you take this view, that *dharma* has no ego, you will realize that there is no true shape in *dharma* and there is no fixed performance in *dharma*. In Zen when you are given the koan, "When the master shows the fan [68]," the master may ask you how you use it. One may answer by fanning himself; another by using the fan as a ruler. A third may make a tray with it to offer a penny to a beggar. So there is no fixed usage in any article. This is non-ego in *dharma*. According with this, the Buddhist realizes the Mahayana point of view and destroys all those fixed concepts.

A concept is a particular view. A handkerchief is the color white, but really the handkerchief is not white. Looked at in one light, it is gray; in another it is pink. It is all colors, according to the light. There is no such thing as "white"; white is a concept. The human idea of time is also like this—one, two, three, four hours—it is a human concept. When you are amusing yourself, time flies like a streak; but when you are bored to death, ten minutes is like ten years. There is no particular time that has a particular duration. The bodhisattva takes this view of non-ego in *dharma*, and he destroys all concepts.

So how should we act in daily life according to the faith of non-ego? This is one of the great questions. If there is no ego in me, no ego in society, no ego in morality—"I don't care if my neck is cut off" — and if there is no ego in him—"I don't cut his neck off"—there is no war. So how do we use this theory of non-ego? In Nature, when the spring comes. it blooms; when autumn comes, it dries. When the wind blows, waves appear. When the stream comes to rapids, there is a waterfall. We must feel such changes within ourselves. When spring comes, how do we feel and how do we act? When autumn comes, what changes will come in our physical body and our mental body? So we must realize by our own experience how this non-ego performs within us. We are hungry when swimming. We see a big fish, and we catch it, put it in a pot, cook it, and eat it. Is there any ego in the human mind? We call it, in Buddhist terms, *asamskrita*—no artificiality. Yet, when we have a little room in the autumn, we like to buy artificial flowers; we like to see their little permanence. So this artificiality must be accepted as one of the performances of Nature.

When you truly understand non-ego, you will find your freedom in every place and at every time. To find your emancipation in every place is called *pratimoksha*.

Find emancipation in every circumstance, in every moment, and in every place.

# KARMA

What is karma? Karma is really action for a purpose—action to attain something, or do something. The suggested meaning in early Buddhism is "purposeful action for some ulterior motive." You are eating food, for instance, but you eat more than you need, so you become ill, thus receiving the result caused by eating too much. It is like not going to bed at night, then being fatigued and unable to work the next day. Or, if when you are walking on the street you hit someone and get knocked down, your being knocked down is the result of karma. Not knowing the law of Nature, the law of sentient beings, you have created or received karma. Buddhism enlarged upon this idea, and developed it into the theory of creative law. Perhaps the Buddha had some such idea, but it does not appear in the early sutras. In them, "purposely" implies an ulterior motive. The result of karmic action may be received in this world, or in the next. Reincarnation is not only of the body, but of the thoughts. My thoughts came from my teacher, and now they are transmitted to you. With these thoughts I act one way, you another.

The idea of *samsara* makes an entirely different point. When a person dies, it is the end of individuality, not of life; it is an air bubble coming up from the pond. For a time the bubble keeps its shape and stays a little while reflecting all, then bursts and disappears. All returns and all will be annihilated. Though the universe is destroyed, original nature is not. From emptiness the body of power is created, and this power creates vibration. Vibration creates heat and motion. After the destruction of the universe, the solar system, lower sentient beings, plants, animals, and man return exactly as before. It may be a million years later, but in infinity this is just a moment, like the thoughts in the mind that come and go. In deep meditation you can experience the thread of light that comes and goes in a repeated rhythm. You can feel it in yourself, and you feel it is in the universe as it is in you. This essential element keeps all seeds. Nothing is destroyed. Simply, this is the theory of *samsara*.

Karma is of the body, the lips, and the mind. "Do not kill," the Buddha told his disciples. "Do not steal. Do not commit adultery." These karmas belong to the body. To kill for sport is a pastime in America, as it was in the ancient days of Japan. The samurai wishing to test a new sword would hide in some dark corner of the street and wait for someone to approach. Perhaps it was an old mother going to arrange her daughter's marriage. "Haaaaaaaaaa!" and he killed her. "How wonderful this sword is!" he says. Today, too, when someone kills an enemy, he laughs. Do not take what is not permitted, not given to you. When you see something beautiful and attach to it, that is stealing. Attachment is stealing. Nothing really belongs to any particular person. When the time comes, all goes with the body, which also does not belong to you.

# THE THREE WORLDS

When the Buddha described the three worlds, he made them a staircase of meditation to ascend to *nirodha-samadhi*, the *samadhi* of complete annihilation. The three worlds, explained by a metaphor, are like an egg. The yolk is *kamadhatu*, the white is *rupadhatu*, and the outside of the shell is *arupadhatu*. In the center of the yolk is *naraka*—hell. The outside disappears into the chaos of the infinite. So sentient minds have hell in the center.

The *Lotus Sutra* [69] says the three worlds, like burning houses, are not places where you can stay forever. So what are they? The worlds of desire, appearance, and non-appearance—*kamadhatu*, *rupadhatu*, and *arupadhatu*. A complete description of the three worlds is given in the *Abhidharmakosha-bhashya* [70].

In the world of *kamadhatu*, sentient beings live in desire. In the world of *rupadhatu*, sentient beings live in the senses. In the world of *arupadhatu*, sentient beings live in pure consciousness. Sentient beings who live in the three worlds, according to their own karma that they produced in the past, chose their dwelling place and must live there, whether they like it or not. When the Buddha said, "Do not attach to the desire to stay in the three worlds," he was handling the idea negatively, saying the desire for *kamadhatu*, the desire for *rupadhatu*, and the desire for *arupadhatu* must be abandoned.

The word *kama* comprises several meanings, such as "desire," "intention," "purpose." In the world of *kamadhatu*, sentient beings always have desire, such as to eat, to generate, etc. And, according to their type of desire, there are five kinds of sentient beings—demons, animals, hungry ghosts, human beings, and pure beings. Of course, you must not think that the sentient beings living in the world of desire are sinful or impure. Desire is the condition of the sentient beings. It is like having your clothes wet when you are on the beach—it is a condition of being on the beach. There is water there, and you cannot do anything about it. You mustn't misunderstand the nature of desire in the world of *kamadhatu*. It is not your desire or my desire; it is the desire of Great Nature. We have nothing to do with our desire, but we can do nothing without it. When we observe human life, it must be from that angle.

In the world of *rupadhatu* we are in the world of "form," "body," and "phenomena." All that we can perceive with our senses is called *rupa*, from the four great elements—earth, air, fire, and water—to the atomic elements of thoughts that haunt our mind. The sense organs of touch, taste, and smell really belong to the world of desire, while the organs of the eye and ear function in the world of appearance or form.

We can draw a line between the world of desire and the world of appearance in our lives. When I look at a lady's dress, I see its beauty, but my mind does not desire it. I am, therefore, living in the world of appearance, not the world of desire. When an artist sees the statue of the Venus de Milo, he perceives the beauty of the form, but it does not arouse the usual conception of woman in his mind. In this case, his mind is entirely isolated from the world of desire. He is in the world of appearance only. An English word applies here—aesthetics.

Our sense of taste, however, sometimes isolates itself from the idea of eating, or the idea of eating from the desire to eat. A wine-taster tastes "purely" and has no desire to drink the wine. He may be completely intoxicated at the end of the day, of course, but his mind remains on the taste, the pure taste of the wine, and he has no desire for it. But at the end of the day he may go home and ask his wife to go to the corner to buy him a bottle of cheap wine to drink with his dinner. He drinks the cheap wine with great pleasure. Here, he is in the world of desire, but his purely tasting wine is in the world of appearance. The story of Pygmalion is a good illustration. Pygmalion, who carved from pure delight in seeing (in *rupadhatu*), fell into the world of desire (*kamadhatu*) when he fell in love with his own handiwork. So the lower sense organs cannot always be placed in the world of desire.

Rupa, therefore, does not include the state of Reality, but it does include the states of all phenomena—seeing, hearing, smelling, tasting, touching, and thinking, but especially seeing. Seeing in rupa has nothing to do with desire, has nothing to do with keeping the seed or nursing it, or educating, or creating, or recreating. It is just seeing. This seeing is a wonderful thing. Without it, we would never see the conclusion of our thoughts. Of course, hearing is very important, too. Somewhere in the sutras the Buddha said, "In this world, hearing is the highest sense [71]." Hakuin [72] showed his hand and said, "Can you hear the sound of a single hand?" Hear the sound of a single hand! When you hear the sound of a single hand you can hear the endless sound that was never created and will never vanish. This enlightenment comes through the ear, not the eye. I cannot see the Buddha now, but through my ear I realize Buddha. Through my ear he is standing here beside me, and he is talking to me, and I am answering him. We understand all the Buddha's teaching through the ear. It has been said that hearing is the first virtue. So for Zen students, seeing is the first virtue. Do not forget that! In Zen you can look at Reality; therefore, seeing is the first virtue. But in arupadhatu, the world of non-seeming, non-appearance, non-form, we can see many things our eye cannot see, hear what our ear cannot hear.

One day when I was struggling to understand Buddhism and I was thinking about the arupadhatu because I did not understand what it was, I all of a sudden burst into it. Then the whole system of Buddhism became clear to my mind. I thought I would like to see this world, and I came to see it. To each student there is some gate through which he breaks into the main avenue. I entered through the gate which is called arupadhatu.

The heretics (as the many sects contemporary with the Buddha were called) believed that arupadhatu was the highest abode, the highest state the student could attain. Following Udraka Ramaputra, one of the Buddha's teachers, Buddha himself attained this state; but realizing that *arupadhatu* was also a kind of attachment, he threw *arupadhatu* overboard and entered *nirodha-samadhi*, absolute annihilation. Henceforth, in Buddhism absolute annihilation was the highest subject that the student had to comprehend.

*Arupadhatu* is the purely mental, metaphysical world. There is nothing that has form in it, but it is not absolutely empty; there are thoughts in this state. A sentient being in *arupadhatu* has no body, no purpose, no intention. But he has his own invisible body. The sentient being who lives in this world conceives nothing but infinite space. His empty consciousness enters into *akasha*. Meditating upon this infinite space, he realizes duration, and realizes that space has time. Space is not merely an extension but has duration, and it is not only horizontal extension, but extends perpendicularly as time. Consciousness enters time as my foot enters my shoe and realizes that it has life, realizing space and time as its own extension. It is not material, objective existence. Space and time are its own expression of its own constituents. In this endless space and time, one meditates, and forgets one's own existence. This is the third world.

In the world of *arupadhatu*, space is a mirror, and time is a mirror. Reflecting each other, they reflect no shadows between them; there is no consciousness here. Forgetting your own conscious existence, consciousness falls into absolute oblivion, forgetfulness. But from this forgetfulness, this emptiness, consciousness revives once more. Through time and space, it rises and realizes the existence of the entire three worlds. However, you are not creating or thinking about this entire existence—you possess all three worlds in your own nature. Therefore, this place, the highest place in *arupadhatu* is called "neither thought nor no-thought." As I said, some Buddhist schools place one more state upon this and call it *nirodha-samadhi*, absolute annihilation, but it is different from the absolute emptiness in the third stage of *arupadhatu*.

There is endless material in these three worlds, but I am presenting just an outline. I am sorry if it is so awfully complicated, but there is no other way of explaining it in this kind of popular lecture.

One last thing. Buddhists must not think that mind is included in this body. Our mind is not living in this body. Our mind is not living in this skull. This skull is just like a radio apparatus. Our mind is always living in the Great Universe. When I walk, I walk with the universe. When I think, I think with the Great Universe, not with this little skull. This thinking capacity is not my own; it is not my mind that thinks, it is the Mind of the Universe—a very mysterious world. It is not that I think about sixty years, and after death I don't think anymore. No. When you consider this carefully, this is the great performance, the great drama of sentient beings in which we are all taking part. When you see Tibetan paintings of monks performing ancient works of art in different kinds of masks, you are seeing the symbols of all kinds of sentient beings and the different ways they see things. This makes a wonderful drama, and we are acting in it every day.

# THE FIVE WAYS OF KAMADHATU

Today, I shall tell you about the five ways (*panca-gati*) of sentient beings in the world of desire, *kamadhatu*, the first of the three worlds. The five ways of sentient beings are *naraka, tiryagyoni, preta, manusya,* and *deva* [73]. All these beings, not only human beings, but all sentient beings, are reborn mentally and physically according to their past karma, the actions committed by their body, mind, and speech. Sometimes the five ways are referred to as "evil" ways. Why are human beings and *devas* also referred to as evil? Compared with the state of the Pure Land [74], the five ways are evil ways.

*The Way of Hell*
Sentient beings are born in Hell (*naraka*) according to the evil karma committed by them in the past. Hell is the most abased state in the *kamadhatu*, the lowest in the worlds of desire. Of the three worlds, *kamadhatu* is the lowest, and *naraka* is the lowest in *kamadhatu*. Hell is subjective, not objective. It does not exist under the ground; it is the subconscious state. It is the agony that you feel in your mind as a result of your past karma. It is the place of atonement. The *Abhidharma* says: "Why do you call *naraka* the place of atonement? Because there is no pleasure, no joy; because there is no way out; because there is no virtue and no way of disengaging yourself from karma. Therefore, it is called the dungeon of the subterranean regions." Of course, from an intellectual point of view it is the state of affliction, what is called *vikalpa-klesha*, "the agony of erroneous views," the lowest activity in our life. When you commit murder, your mind falls into the state of torment. This is a natural law. If you commit willful murder, inevitably you will fall into the fear that other sentient beings will not permit you to exist. As a result, you must bear

feelings of fear and torment. When your imagination creates a hypothesis, you compare this hypothesis with reality, then take the answer inferred from the hypothesis as true. Usually *vikalpa* is translated as "conjecture," and *klesha* as "affliction," or "suffering," the suffering that haunts the *skandha* of *samskara*. *Vikalpa* are the conjectures that appear in the shadow *samjna*. *Klesha* are the subconscious sufferings, while *vikalpa* are the conscious sufferings. Conjectures, imagination, superstitions, are considered the state of hell—in one word, *vikalpa-klesha*.

To control and eradicate *vikalpa-klesha* is the purpose of our meditation. We eradicate it to attain the state of mind without affliction. There is no way out of hell, but you will find the way out by meditation. Indeed, there is no joy or pleasure in hell; it is a place no one wants to fall into. And you cannot find the way out by yourself; someone must make a way for you. Dwellers in these hells are isolated from the society of human beings. They are in a snowbound country and want to reach out to others in distant lands, but they are in isolation.

By the way, in the East you don't "go" to hell; you "fall" into hell.

### The Way of Horizontal-Goers

*Tiryagyoni*, "the way of beasts," is the second of the five ways of sentient beings. *Tir* means "horizon"; *yoni* means "kind." So those who walk "horizontally" are called *tiryagyoni*. While we walk upright, standing on our feet, animals walk horizontally. The name, therefore, includes all kinds of beasts, birds, and insects. The characteristics of the species in this state is that they harm each other. The stronger ones devour the weaker. According to their karma, they bear many agonies.

Those who devour weaker ones without mercy are counted as *tiryagyoni*, thus falling after death into this state. Though they possess the form of human beings, they live the life of beasts. Why? Because they lack sympathy and love. In their next reincarnation they will bear endless agony. Stupidity is the cause. Without knowledge they cannot see the world of love, sympathy, or compassion. They use and exploit others to satisfy their own ego and desires. They go astray because they have no knowledge, and they return to original darkness, broken from bearing heavy burdens. They cannot raise themselves to see the sun of enlightenment. Under their heavy burdens they give up the life of enlightenment. All such beings, whether in the form of beasts or men are horizontal-goers.

In the sutras we are told to pray for the beasts, that they may attain awakening in their beast minds. So this state is not only a physical state, but also a psychological one.

There are five causes for human beings to fall into the way of beasts: stealing, debt, murder, not going to the temple, and calamity.

*The Way of Pretas*
If you keep food in your storehouse and someone who is starving begs food from you, and because of your miserly nature you refuse the request, you will as a result forget your own store of food. Even though you are surrounded by food and wealth, you will forget the existence of your own wealth, and you will forget how to turn it into food. You will have fallen into the state of hunger, the state called *preta*. So when you wish to eat, and someone offers you food, because of your suspicious mind you will be unable to take it. You say, "Take it away! You are trying to poison me!" Or, if you are offered a good chance in business, you say, "Don't think I'm such a fool; you can't trick me!" In such way you will lose many opportunities. Because of your past karma you cannot believe in your present circumstances, so you fall into calamity.

The word *preta* comes from the Sanskrit word *pitri*, meaning "father," which comes from the name Rajapitri, which appears in the Vedas [75]. Its meaning is "grandfather," the first to die in the past world, the one before this present world. Yama, Rajapitri's son, was the first to die in this present world. He is the king of *pretas* and appears in the pictures of hell. According to legend, those who die childless become hungry *pretas* after their death because they have no children to offer them food or water on the anniversary of their death. When negligent children forget and fail to offer their parents something to eat or drink, the parents will starve in *yama-loka* [76] and become hungry *pretas*. So in filial piety it is important for children to remember their dead parents.

Sentient beings in the state of *preta* see food, but cannot eat. They see delicious food that invites their appetite with fragrant aromas, beautiful soft colors, and chopsticks beside it, but their minds prevent them from eating. They think something will happen to them if they do, so they starve looking at it. A friend invites him to dinner, cordially prepares special food, buys new utensils and new chopsticks. When the *preta* comes to the table, he cries, "You are trying to poison me!" So the friend never invites him again. The *preta* forgets the value of food and even the words "food" and "water." Not in a thousand years will he be able to recall not only the words but their appearance. Though he sees water with his eyes, he will not realize it is the very thing that will quench his thirst. In his oblivion he has forgotten how to drink, and so he suffers eternally.

There was once a monk who lost his way in a great western desert. After some time he went down into a cavity of the earth. In the depths of the cavern he found five hundred *pretas* scratching in agony. When the monk shouted, "Water!" they cried, "That's it! That's the name we forgot!"

This is an allegory, of course, of the human being born in this world who cannot recall the name of Buddha. He feels something lacking in himself. He feels he needs something. There is something empty in his mind, so he tries to recall an old memory. He tries to remember some old teaching, but he fails. He thinks it's money, so he looks for money. He thinks it's love, so he loves a woman. But he fails to find what he is looking for. He does not realize that what he is looking for is his original nature.

Some *pretas* eat fire and are satisfied, but to eat fire it must throw itself into fire. This kind of *preta* is called a "fiery moth." Some pretas have stomachs swollen like mountains, and throats as thin as needles, so they cannot eat. These *pretas* live everywhere, and they usually give their service to the Four Maharajas who stand at the four corners of the universe. They run around the world as their messengers. Or, they find new ways to reach other places, as their forefather found the way to reach hell. Sometimes they live in nice places, and in beautiful countries. Sometimes they live in the dung-pots of hell.

I must make a remark here. In the stories of pretas there are many elements having to do with food, but one never finds any element of sex. Of course, these days when a man is crazy about a woman, we say he is a "sex-*preta*." And some *pretas* metamorphose themselves to engender their own kind; others conceive babies just as human beings do.

A *preta* in the stage of starvation suffers in body and mind, and the body and mind tortures the soul and drives it out. All those whose karma has been marked by avarice, cruelty, and miserliness fall into this state after death.

There are two kinds of *pretas*—dignified and undignified. Their occupation is that of gate guard, follower, or messenger. Some *pretas* enjoy their lives, like *devas*. Others are tormented like dead spirits in hell. Though they are enjoying themselves, as *pretas* they must live with other *pretas* who are suffering. However, the dignified *pretas* can never really live entirely separated from the undignified ones. When we see pictures of *rakshasas* [77] walking through the heavens like angels, we can see little *pretas* with black skins alongside them. The *pretas* are just skin and bone and ligaments. The dignified *pretas* cannot drive them away, but must speak to them as equals. While *devas* walk through the world of *kamadhatu* and speak to those of the other ways, the *pretas* must speak to all the demons underground and even in hell. Pretas are always vomiting fire from their throats, because they have always vomited evil words from their mouths. Some *pretas* have needles for hair on their bodies. Some *pretas* are visible, some invisible. Sometimes the human mind is possessed by a *preta* and acts like a *preta*. As the invisible *preta* cannot act by itself, it enters the human mind and possesses it. So it is through human beings that *pretas* attain their malicious ways.

When the Buddha gives a sermon, all the bodhisattvas come, and in the background are eight kinds of supernatural beings: 1) *yakshas*—violent, malignant beings; 2) *nagas*—rain dragons; 3) *gandharvas*—heavenly musicians; 4) *ashuras*—angry demons; 5) *kinnaras*—musicians sometimes described as having men's bodies and horses' heads; 6) *garudas*—a kind of bird; 7) *mahoragas*—dragons like boa-constrictors; 8) and *devas*. There are also monsters, such as the *kumbhandas*. When Buddhism is supported, the eight kinds of supernatural beings and monsters support it first.

When I was ordained a Zen master by my teacher, one of my brothers said to me: "Your teacher ordained you a monk, but all the eight groups of demons must ordain you, too. Otherwise you cannot be a perfect monk."

I am expecting them!

### The Way of Human Beings

*Manusya* are sentient beings who think. Of course, there are other meanings that are carried over into the Chinese translations, such as "arrogance" from the Sanskrit word *mana*, which means "pride." Sentient beings living in this state are prideful and arrogant. The most arrogant of sentient beings is man. But this translation is not correct. Sometimes it is translated as from the word *manas* (mind), implying that it is the state of mind, not the activity of mind. *Manas* is mind or will-power, but "man" is "the action of mind," "to think"; therefore, we take this word from *manu*, to think. So *manusya* is one who thinks, the estate of the being human. We are all acquainted with this state as we are in it at this very moment. But eccentric men try to get out and think they somehow can succeed in doing so. They stay in mountain caves and meditate years, but they are entirely deluded. Some of them meditate upon cliffs believing they will someday attain the power to fly through the sky, but their dream will be destroyed in mid-air. They will fall and die. So as long as you are in the state of *manusya*, you must decide to live in this body and mind. This decision is a fundamental truth in Buddhism.

## The Way of Devas

*Deva* means "joy"; *devaloka* means "place of joy." *Deva* comes from the Sanskrit root *div*, which means "to shine. *Deva* is also used in words for "god," or the "place of gods." The place were *devas* live is sometimes called "the beautiful and excellent world." Here there will be no agony by which all other sentient beings are tormented. The state of *deva* contains something of the idea of Greek Idealism. The state of *deva* is the highest, most joyous, most beautiful and good. Those who in previous lives were obedient to all rules of virtue and perfectly behaved themselves in body, mind, and speech will continue their lives in that state. Of course, in light of the experience of meditation, this state is a state of mind, not a physical state. It does not exist in material space but in mental space. *Devaloka* is a space experienced in meditation.

# THE FOUR HEAVENS OF RUPADHATU

When the stages of *rupadhatu* are explained legendarily, they appear as the mythology of Buddhism. In the early days, Western scholars failed to grasp what Buddhism was talking about. They thought Buddhists were talking about gods and goddesses, like the gods and goddesses of Greek mythology. They explained *rupadhatu* as they explained Mt. Olympus in Greek mythology—Jupiter, Eros, and Diana on a mountaintop. No wonder they failed to understand Buddhism! No wonder they put no emphasis upon the three worlds. This means, of course, they failed to grasp *dhyana*—meditation itself, the core of Buddhism.

Meditation on the four *dhyana-lokas*, the four stages of meditation in the *rupadhatu*, is entirely in the sphere of aesthetics. No meditation is based on the desire realm of *kamadhatu*. In some sects of Buddhism, the *samadhi* of desire is accepted as a kind of *dhyana*, but the duration of this *samadhi* is very short. Its duration is as short as a burning drop of liquor touching your tongue—a moment of ecstasy. In that moment you are in *samadhi*, but it is ephemeral and is not a true state of meditation. However, the *samadhi* of the *kamadhatu* is widely known in the theory of meditation, so I mention it here.

The first stage of *dhyana* in the *rupadhatu* makes use of our present reason with definite intention, conscious effort, and concentration. This is brain power operating on some problem. When this effort becomes feeble, the brain itself continues to carry on its function without your conscious aim—this is inspiration.

The second stage of *dhyana* in the *rupadhatu* appears in your mind as a dream. Your mind functions without your aid. It is a non-intentional state of *dhyana*. It appears in the first part of the second stage when the meditator relinquishes all words and then all images.

Words are the instruments of reasoning, and when we dream, we dream in mental images. We relinquish both words and images in this meditation and we feel that our body becomes quite light, as though we were in midair. Our brain stops operating and reasoning. At this time the body starts to quiver, convulsions come here and there, our eyelids twitch, our lips move by themselves, and often our knees start to shake. Sometimes people become frightened of this queer physical condition and get up and stop their meditation. This is a sign that conscious intention is fading, and the force of Nature is taking its place. Our body is supported by our intention. Holding our mind by our own conscious intention, we are concentrating to attain our desire. So when this intention is abandoned, Nature takes over— our own egoistic intention disappears. In that moment you will feel physical disturbances and twitches all over your body, and your heart will beat in a rhythm you cannot stop. You are as if possessed. You will try to lift your hand, but it is so heavy you cannot. Your tongue becomes big, and you hear sounds as if at a distance. These are some of the usual signs of the second stage, but this is not a true stage at all, and they are only passing phenomena.

In the third stage we come to bliss.

Then we enter the fourth stage of *dhyana*—we forget ourselves. We are not sleepy, but we are completely relaxed and abandoned; we are embraced by Nature, by universal force. We are fused with the universe, and our consciousness is all-pervading, universal consciousness. Our individual self, individual consciousness, is completely wiped out, and Nature operates the functions of our mind, of which we are conscious. In just that moment, those who have trained themselves for a long time in Buddhism will attain enlightenment. I call this the "hairpin turn," as, in the Catskills, I come to a road and go to the peak, then turn, and then return from the peak [78]. When we forget ourselves and abandon ourselves entirely to Nature, the great force of Nature operates our functions and our sense perceptions. Our performance at that moment is not our own. Our self is completely wiped out. We are submerged, absorbed in the bosom of Nature. So-called enlightenment comes at this moment. But some people will miss that moment. They will come back again from it and drink their tea, or go out and eat their breakfast. It's as if you went into a dragon's cave and came out without ever having met the dragon. If, at that moment, at the hairpin turn, you have no penetrating intellectual force with which to reach nirvana, there is no other force which can break through the film of original darkness or ignorance into nirvana. Without grasping nirvana, you are therefore pushed by the power of Nature back into this world.

Empirically speaking, the experience of the meditator is that of being completely abandoned by the clouds of desire. All the clouds produced by fire do not reach to this heaven. The ingrained habits or anxieties of the lower stages are completely destroyed here, and one is released and emancipated completely from the lower heavens and is reborn in a new state of spirit. When you reach here, you reach the bottom of meditation. However, you will want to come back again. You will want to return as quickly as a diver from the bottom of the sea. But it is usually without attaining nirvana, enlightenment, without seeing the dragon of the Dragon Cave, that men come back.

But if you continue on, you will reach a place where there are no disturbances of reasoning or of desire; no disturbance of either *vedana* or *samjna*. All disturbances that come from the senses and all thoughts are wiped away.

It is the complete annihilation of thought. Here you are already embraced in the bosom of God, and your sight has been kindled so that you see all the phenomena of heaven. You see the phenomena of a higher stage than the world. This means that you revive and see this marvelously manifested world from its roots.

# THE FOUR REALMS OF ARUPADHATU

In the sphere of *arupadhatu* there is nothing which can be thought or seen. This is the nature of this state of meditation. When I first heard of *arupadhatu* meditation I immediately thought it cannot be concrete truth, for human beings cannot refuse that which can be seen by eyes; cannot escape from our consciousness. I realized that the *arupadhatu* doctrine is pure hypothesis, that it cannot be accepted as fact. I'm quite sure Shakyamuni Buddha also realized this in some such fashion, as I did.

You must understand that I am merely giving you a lecture on the theory of *arupadhatu*, that I am not insisting that this *arupadhatu* theory is true, and that I am not imposing it on you, or that you practice it. Buddhism is absolutely a theory, and Zen is a practice to introduce you to truth, to carry you into the state of realization. While you are observing koans or listening to lectures you cannot perceive in haste what Buddhism is, or arrive at any conclusion about it. I remind you of this point. The theory of *arupadhatu*, however, has some importance. In the concrete sense, it is not entirely hypothesis. It is one of the great divisions of Buddhist theory.

In *arupadhatu* there are four stages. When the meditator has abstracted every thought and every form of existence, he will find himself in boundless space. To you, space extends before your eyes; to us, space extends within our minds. You try to retreat to a place quiet on the outside. We try to attain quietude within our minds. What disturbs our mind is thoughts. Thoughts are temporary phenomena. Of course with these thoughts comes violent emotion which has disturbing force. In meditation the Zen student tries to conquer this. That is our discipline. We cannot live always in such a fashion because we must live as human beings, but fundamentally our minds must take root in immobile mind. Without finding yourself in this first stage you cannot find yourself in absolute quietude.

In the second stage of *arupadhatu*, the meditator finds himself in his own consciousness. Until this time the meditator thought that *he* was the center of an immense universal space. But that universal space was not space; it was the sphere of his own consciousness. Consciousness means duration. It has no extension, but it has duration. Duration means time, that is, the duration of all life. It means the life of the soul. Of course in that *samadhi* the meditator does not abstract space; he finds time within space. This space, however, is not so-called geometrical space, but so-called time-space. These days Western people talk about time-space, or space-time, and they call it the fourth dimension. To explain it they apply higher mathematics; we simply apply our meditation to solve that question of time-space.

In the third stage, having acquainted himself with endless time, the meditator disappears. He buries himself in the *samadhi* of meditation. It is like a deep sleep. In deep sleep, you know, you disappear, and until you wake up you cannot find yourself between heaven and earth. Absolutely disappeared! In meditation, it is the same.

It is by observation in meditation that we cultivate the power of concentration on the fragments of our thoughts. When I was young, I paid no attention to my subconscious mind, never knew what was going on in it. But later, when I was older and paid attention to it, I carefully penetrated some considerable depth into it. The subconscious mind is absolutely uncontrollable, but sometimes by concentration it is possible to penetrate into it. When your conscious mind penetrates to your subconscious mind, then you forget yourself and there is no space or time left.

As I've said, in the third stage of *arupadhatu* meditation you are absolutely wiped out. But do not make the hasty conclusion that this is the last stage. It looks that way. But even though we Buddhists would say that your *samadhi* is quite deep, your practice is not good enough. You think there will be no thoughts, no law, no space, no time, no crystallized operation of mind. But that is erroneous. When you reach the absolute state, you will find the law of mind. Until that time you are bothered by something else, and you cannot find the law of mind written in your own mind. So those heretics get lost because they cannot find the law within themselves. But when you begin to realize that mind operates in that bottomless nothing, too, and is a kind of crystallized form, then you will realize that mind-itself is always trying to find a balance. In this present consciousness, balance can be manifested as moral law. But in the primary state, it appears as balance. Great Life in this universe has this rhythm. You call it vibration as it balances. It is natural. There is no dead emptiness in nirvana, as your philosophers think. So those of you who drop into the dead emptiness of Buddhism don't know Buddhism.

In deep *samadhi*, when our own mind ceases to exist, our mind is switched to the Great Universe. Its rhythm is not coarse, like our usual thinking, but this state of nothingness is not dead; it is living. Then, for the first time, the individual ego makes contact with the Great Ego of the Universe, and the small ego surrenders before this Great Ego.

This connection is religion. You may put on robes and you may put a diploma before your shrine and talk about religion, but if you have not had this connection, you cannot call yourself a religious man. Before you surrender you are so small, and you try to do every-thing against the force of Great Nature. "Well," you say, "If I follow this teaching I will be like those who follow blind nature. I will become like an animal. Perhaps following that religion I will become greedy, passionate, immoral." No, that is your ignorance. We are not obeying human nature. We are not taking orders from human imag-ination. We learn the true order, the true rhythm, the true vibration, the true law of Nature.

When you see snow through a microscope, this nice, hard snow, how beautiful it is! The law of crystallization is operating in it. There is negative crystallization; there is also positive crystallization. The tree gets warped and distorted by the wind and the sun, the environ-ment, but the nature of the tree is to be symmetrical, so it is always striking a balance with its branches — this way, that way. In meditation you find that law within your heart. Perhaps you are painting a picture —here you put a little bird, there something else — you are striking a balance, aren't you? If you do not feel that law you are not an artist. And in the human law of daily life, in the relations of men and women, this law of crystallization also operates. If you don't see it, are blind to it, you are indeed like an animal. We are all like a tree that is warped and distorted, but we are not naturally so terribly twisted and distorted. We must know where this queer distortion comes in to our life, must find out where it begins. So we go back.

The fourth stage in *arupadhatu* is not thoughts but it is not no-thoughts. It is neither thinking nor no-thinking. It is not thoughts such as you now have, thinking everything with your mind. That thinking is called coarse thoughts, untrained thoughts, ordinary thoughts. When you switch yourself to Great Nature, thoughts are there, but they are different from your usual thoughts.

So refusing to see anything, to hear anything, and keeping the mind as quiet as stagnant water might be the law of the ascetic, but it is not the attitude of the Buddha. The Buddha's attitude was entirely different from that of the sages of his time. They were living in mountain caves, drinking from streams and eating wild berries, living between life and death. Their bodies were emaciated, and their view narrow. He, too, was called a sage, but his attitude was entirely different from theirs. He brought the law of the mountaintop into everyday life. He extended the Law which operates in crystallization into the law of human life.

# THE ONE OF MYSTERIOUS PURPORT

Have you ever wondered why the Buddha is shown seated or standing upon a hundred-petaled lotus? Everything great in Nature has its softness, its elasticity. The lotus is not like metal or wood but like soil and air; it is very soft, and this softness is the ground that makes it great and indestructible. Softness is the symbol of Earth, the Mother Earth that includes everything and produces everything. When we manifest this mysterious power that has been bestowed upon us by Her, we use soft mind, not sharp or hard mind. We use soft, meek mind.

There are many colorful personalities among human beings. Some are wise, some are sharp, some like sculptures, and some like paintings. The most wonderful are like music. They have a wonderful, intrinsic rhythm of Nature about them, and there is always softness in their hearts. Of course, someone who has no courage to do anything is meek. This is not wonderful, however. But if it is a wonderful meekness, it is not proud against the great power of the universe; it is wonderful. The Bible says, "Blessed are the meek, for they shall inherit the earth." That is why the Buddha, manifesting all the mysteries of the universe, is shown seated upon the lotus.

However, what we see with our eyes is not soft, comparatively speaking. What I am talking about is like very pure air, like mist—everything reduced to the oneness of existence. If you expand yourself to the ends of the universe, you will not feel anything; you will see yourself in the even course of the universe. Of course, you can do this only if you realize that your ego is not yours. So it is through the awareness that your ego is not yours that you can expand into the oneness that is the great storehouse of universal manifestation. In Buddhism everything is born out of this great oneness, this infinite oneness, and this oneness is empty, but it conceives all seeds. It conceives everything. When all things disappear from our eyes but remain in the oneness of form and color, it is like the conservation of energy. THAT is not there. THAT is in us, here. The Great Softness, the Great White Lotus, is here in us.

The lotus is also the symbol of our heart, and our heart is the symbol of the universe. The heart is the microcosm. As the universe produces everything, our heart also produces everything. Our heart produces happiness, misery, whatever you want. This heart is also soul. The brain is also soul, but the heart does not reason. This is the wonderful part. To the Buddhist the brain seems cheap, reasoning everything. So the knowledge of the brain is not so wonderful. The heart's knowledge is different, however. Reason is like using a small knife, but the heart, without reasoning, manifests all mystery. The heart as soul is called *hridaya* in Sanskrit, but the soul that is active in the brain is called *citta* [79], and their natures are very different.

Have you ever seen anything similar to the heart, with the lungs covering it and all the veins running through the body? There is a fundamental and primitive form of life that lives exactly like the heart and lungs, a soul that is without reasoning. Wonderful trees are like that. Observe the heart and lungs and you will realize the life of the tree in us, which is like the life of the tree in the air. If you had heart only and no brain, your soul would be at the same stage as the tree. Observe the leaves of a tree; they are the lungs of the heart. Its small cells are taking in air and discharging gas. The heart is a tree-minded being living in our body, just like *citta* living in our soul. The *citta* in the brain makes too much trouble, but without a heart we could not live. Can you imagine a universe that had no brain function but is just the life of the heart expanding through the universe? We call it "The Universe of the Lotus Womb World." This womb produces all the mysterious forms of existence. So trees have no individuality. They have different shapes, but their souls are all the same. We, however, are so selfish we perceive very differently. We perceive according to our desire. Therefore, there is trouble.

*We* are the Lotus. All trees are the Lotus. All stars are the Lotus. The sun and moon are the Lotus. All life, not reasoning but living in the harmony of the one great universal power, is the Lotus. All are in different shapes, of course, but the heart is one. In the sky there are millions of Lotus worlds; the ocean is a million lotus-hearted worlds, and not one million but infinite millions.

If you understand this, what is your question? After your death your soul will return to the pure ocean of the lotus-hearted universe. You are one with the universe in that stage but also part of it, because the "you" returns to pure existence. If the soul that returns to the root could not come back, we could not conceive the same thing again. Our mind repeats life and death every moment. Our blood runs in rhythm. If we died only once, we could not conceive the same thing in the next moment. I die? No. I sleep tonight, but mysteriously I find myself in this body the next morning. This proves that you conceive the same soul again in your body when your soul returns again. Dust circling in the corner of the street blown by the wind makes the same shape many times. The four great elements compose the old form again anew, the soul within it. You really have to call yourself "The Returned-Again."

The one moon is reflected in a hundred different ricefields lying in tiers on the hillside. Draw a picture in your mind to understand this—ricefields with ridges, and paths to keep the water in. Again and again there are the ridges, tiers on tiers on the hillside. The paddy field was made to keep the water in. When the moon is reflected in every ricefield, in the hundreds of ricefields, there are a thousand different shapes. In the same water the quivering moonprint is shaking, rushing, running. Yet, it is quiet in its round shape. If the water runs off, no moon is reflected.

When Nature composes the universal body, the one universal moon reflects. When the material body is not composed, the moon is not reflected. The body composes anew according to cause and effect, as a sound broadcast returns to the same spot. We are broadcasting karma from morning to evening, and all the records are kept, and again it is composed. The moon reflects that soul, that nameless thing we call soul. Therefore, you can say you have an eternal ego, *atman*, but this is not the Buddhism that emphasizes non-ego, *anatman*. This Buddhism was different from that of the Buddha himself. If there is body and a soul in it, the body will be decomposed and recompose with the same soul. Logically, we can believe this to be so, but if there is no individual ego, there is no need to think about it. A soul is a funny thing; if you look into it, you cannot see it. "Introspect" in meditation, and you will find non-ego, like a fish swimming about, but you will not be able catch it. It's just like calling a cat, "Come here kitty!" and it never comes. Jump on your soul, try to grasp it in meditation, get into it in *samadhi*, and you cannot find it.

Now, speaking about it, I feel there is ego. In Sanskrit, this is called *pudgala* [80], the seed of soul that is combined with body. Then there are the five *skandhas*, the five environments surrounding the soul like fire—purple, orange, red, blue, and white fire—and the seed of fire is there also. Soul combined with body is not soul, not body, not purely spiritual, not purely mental, but existing as the oozing seed of soul that always relates to the material. It carries past karma and transmigrates. It does not go into nirvana, it is not tortured in hell (the state after death in which departed souls are thought to be purified of their past karma). One who has heavy karma transmigrates into a heavy material existence with no freedom, and he is tortured. But good karma bears that which is not so heavy. It is almost pure and not quite so tortured; there is very little experience of purgatory. In such a stage the soul repeats its incarnation.

The Buddha told us that there are mysteries to understand. It is not just that we must find the eternal, universal soul, or that we must find an individual soul. But in between, in everyday life, we must find the individual soul in meditation, find the soul link between the phenomenal and the noumenal, as *sambhogakaya* is the link between *nirmanakaya* and *dharmakaya*. Buddha is under the tree of *nirmanakaya*, but his soul is individual. Buddha is not dead—*sambhogakaya* is always-repeating cause and effect. The ground of *sambhogakaya* eternally exists, not as an individual and not eternally. It has no name. It is like the ocean; it is numberless as the sands of the Ganges. All the seeds of soul come from the same life; there is no individual soul. The whole is *dharmakaya*, the one is *sambhogakaya*; hands and feet and so on are *nirmanakaya*. When the Buddha said, "I was Buddha in a past incarnation," he was speaking of the one of mysterious purport. Yes, he was a reincarnating Buddha, but soul now and soul then was just one soul. Therefore he says, "I was a reincarnating Buddha."

There is a mysterious expression: "If we call upon the name of Amida Buddha, we reach heaven." It is also said: "Through Christ we reach God." It is the same thing. Therefore, through this same thing, we reach the eternal existence of God. This is the mystery.

I took a vow to many Buddhas, and I have been enlightened. I took this vow to as many Buddhas as there are grains of sand in the Ganges. I studied from Hakuin, and I studied from Ma-tsu. In the past I was the student of Kant, Schopenhauer, and Nietzsche. If you understand this, though you die, you are not dead. At the funeral service we see our friend in his coffin. Yesterday he was alive. Today we see him in the deeps of nirvana. He is not dead. All think so, but he is in nirvana, in the Ocean of Soul.

There is nothing so impressive as when you see the death of a friend. The body must be strong, must take shape; then it can be tempered as steel. If it is tempered too much, it will crack. It must be put in the fire again, be made a little soft. Do you believe there is an individual soul or an eternal soul? The soul is but a drop in water; so there is no ego, no individuality. Realize that life and death is nothing but one.

Christ said, "Lazarus, come forth!" and he who was dead came forth. It is not mysterious, not a miracle. It is written plainly, described in the true, honest heart. I understand it very well. To read these words, you must open your eye. Then you will see the mystery.

# THIS IS LIFE AFTER DEATH

Yesterday was such a rainy day. Today is very beautiful. But there was no day between yesterday and today. Sometimes I think this is very strange. When we think of the past and the future, we think the present is an interval, an actuality. But where is this present that the past connects with the future immediately? We do not find any present moment. We say "this moment" on earth, but on Neptune, this moment will be eighty days. Certainly, in eighty days there are many hours and minutes, past and future. If there is no present, logically there will be no past or future; so what are we doing now in this place? Metaphysics always misleads us. It is fine to speak about, but it gives us no substance.

In Buddhism there are two gates. One gate is very sweet, like a honeydew melon. Through this gate, we get art, drama, science, and philosophy. The other gate is the Buddhism that is unspeakable— nothing can be expressed by human words. If I stand upon the angle of this moment, which we cannot place, I must stand in silence—I shall not speak one word to you. When I speak to you, I must speak this beautiful hypothesis. Then Mystery is tangible. I think you will like it when you hear it.

If you were to ask me what happens after death, I would answer: the soul does not die; you will enter a new life, immediately. There is no interval; there is no moment between here and there. When you die, you will reincarnate into new flesh. "New flesh" does not necessarily mean this flesh [designating body], but any flesh which is matter, or a combination of fire, water, earth, and air—all one flesh.

In Buddhism the soul will transmigrate in five ways: demon, animal, hungry ghost, man, and *deva*. But all these stages or ways are really here. "Here" means in this universe, in this city, wherever you are at this moment. *This* is life after death. *This* is delusion—sleeping time. *This* is transitoriness, like the cloud upon the sky—while you are looking at it, it changes its form. We transmigrate while we are sleeping from heaven to hell, from man to beast. When man takes new flesh, it is as if he were operating a radio in Chicago and receiving it here immediately—there is no moment between. This spirit has an orientation within itself; it finds its way and connects according to vibration—where to go according to past karma.

This life is just a dream, so when we really awake from this delusion, from this life of transitoriness, we will enter into eternal life, and there is no death. We have to enter while we are living.

# THIS BUDDHA

In the Buddha's time there was no special name for religion; *dharma* was the name given to all mental activity. Today we divide mental activity into many departments, such as philosophy, science, and all kinds of ideas and isms, as well as religion. The Buddha's Dharma was the practice of no-thinking. Today, we are afraid of that. If we are not thinking something, we believe we will become stupid and return to ignorance, or go back to the age of the caveman. Of course, we cannot avoid thinking, so we must practice to attain the state of no-thinking with this thinking mind. We begin this practice by meditation. But how are we to attain this true attitude of meditation? On what shall we meditate?

First, we meditate on the activity of our eyes, our ears, our mind. We meditate not only upon the human mind but on the mind of trees and weeds, and on the mind of fire, water, and earth. When we meditate upon our own mind, we discover that the mind of the vegetable, which does not think, exists within us. So the no-thinking mind is really within us. We observe this no-thinking mind with our thinking mind. This is the beginning of the practice of meditation.

When I eat my dinner, my thinking mind does not digest it; something else digests it. Some other power pumps my blood and circulates it through my body. My hair and nails do not tell me they grow; they grow while I pay no attention. Something else is living in this body. The part I call myself is only a little part of the whole. I cannot refuse to see without closing my eyes. Whether I want to hear or not, sound vibrates on the drum of my ear. The activities of my eyes and ears do not belong to me; they belong to something within me. So we discover that what we call ourselves, our ego, is a very small part of us. Meditating upon the self, upon the mind, we discover the greater life, and by discovering this greater life, we discover the greater self, the greater mind that can be immediately reached through our own mind. This religion, therefore, has an immediate entrance here. The shrine is right here. Temporarily, I call it Buddha—not the Buddha who was born in India, but the Buddha who exists everywhere. I call it *This* Buddha.

Shakyamuni Buddha decided this was his religion. To us the discovery of this religion by him has great significance. We say that a human being has reached true religion, and that the avenue through which he reached this religion is straight and without hindrance, and you can without doubt have immediate faith in it. Others, however, try to reach something higher than themselves. They are always looking upward and joining their hands. And when they hope to realize something, they offer prayer to someone in the sky. From our standpoint it is not wrong, but it is not very convenient. Why search for it in the sky? Why try to get something you hope for by asking someone else for it? Prayer is the expression of man's immediate desire, and gifts are offered to assure an answer. To us, prayer is our hope, our immediate desire, but we work to get an answer—work, therefore, is our gift. Without the offering of gifts, prayer is not answered. If our desire is natural, it will be answered naturally. If it is unnatural, it will not be answered. We do not need any image to worship. Our self is Buddha, and our mind is the entrance to the shrine of Buddha.

The Buddha's birth brought this religion into the world, and we follow it.

# THE EIGHTEEN SHUNYATAS

The Eighteen Shunyatas is a stiff lecture. I have been teaching for six years in New York [1936], and this is the first time I am speaking about them. These emptinesses are explained by Shakyamuni Buddha in the *Mahaprajnaparamita Sutra*. In this sutra the Buddha said to his disciple Shariputra, "Oh, Shariputra, if you wish to stay within the eighteen *shunyatas*, practice *prajnaparamita*."[81] Emptiness, which is the keystone of Buddhism is the conclusion of this sutra. In it the Buddha was said to have practiced *prajnaparamita* for eight years, and now we have six hundred volumes of what happened.

I hope you will understand this lecture. It is really only for an audience that is expert in Buddhism.

The eighteen *shunyatas* are as follows:

1. Inside is empty.
2. Outside is empty.
3. Inside and outside are empty.
4. Emptiness is empty.
5. The great elements are empty.
6. Reality is empty.
7. Creative purpose is empty.
8. Purposelessness is empty.
9. The conclusion is empty.
10. The beginningless is empty.
11. Undoing phenomena is empty.
12. Your own nature is empty.
13. All existence is empty.
14. One's own appearance is empty.

15. The ungraspable is empty.
16. Non-existence is empty.
17. Existence is empty.
18. Non-existence is empty.

1) The inside is empty (*adhyatma-shunyata*). *Adhyatma* means "one's supreme spirit," the highest spirit of an individual; that individual spirit is empty. According to Buddhism, the inside has six *ayatana* or entrances, five entrances from the outside to the inside. These entrances are the five senses, and one more hidden inside. So altogether there are six senses, and inside is the highest supreme spirit. All are empty, which means there is no ego (*atman*) in it. For example, the eye has no ego, there is no master in it. The ear has no spiritual center, and the rest of the senses have no spiritual centers. So people think the one inner sense is the "king," think it belongs to "you." We Buddhists do not think it is an individual spirit. You think it is yours; but from the Buddhist's standpoint, it is no one's. It is consciousness and consciousness is not yourself. There is no consciousness which is called "you" or "I." So the inside is empty.

2) The outside is empty (*bahirdha-shunyata*). The outside, badhirdha, is the existence opposite to the six senses, something that is other than one's self—color, sound, odor, taste, touch, and semimaterial thoughts, or mind-stuff. Color you can see, like a rainbow, but it is just a vision—it has no real nature. We look at the phenomenal universe as though we were peering into a kaleidoscope; with all noumena, it is just a vision. A scientist would call this vibration. The retina of the eye co-vibrates with the etheric vibrations, and you perceive colors. Colors are not existing outside. The outside is empty.

3) The inside and the outside are empty (*adhyatma-bahirdha-shunyata*). This means that the twelve *ayatana* are empty. The *ayatana* are the eye, ear, nose, mouth, tactual sense, and inner consciousness as well as color, sound, odor, taste, touch, mind-stuff. They are empty. The inside is empty, so the outside is empty. The outside is empty, so the inside is empty. The outside and the inside are empty.

4) Emptiness is empty (*shunyata-shunyata*). When I was young, and I was concentrating on all forms of meditation, one summer I was in the habit of falling into unconsciousness—not sleep, but something like sleep, unconscious of conscious mind. It was a hot summer, and I almost passed away—I had the fear that sometime I would not come back. So when you have emptied the outside and the inside, and find "emptiness," you must empty this conception, as well. With emptiness annihilate emptiness. If you truly understand this, you do not need to take *sanzen* any more.

One day, in Oregon, I went out with my dog on a mountain, and the dog was watching me. I heard the sound of a train, opened my eyes and saw a body. I said, "According to Buddhism, one must one day realize that this body is just a conception." I found my body sitting on a rock with the dog squatting alongside it. Then I heard the whistle of the train and realized that I am empty with all this universe.

This is the first step in Mahayana Buddhism. We do not need to brush all phenomena aside. Of course, if you are a wise one, when you pass a koan, you should realize it. Some of you pass koans just like a donkey passes a fence, but someday you will realize it. Man's conception of Emptiness is Zen, but you must destroy that Zen, too. Then you will find yourself with all the universe. That is *shunyata*.

5) The great elements are empty (*mahashunyata*). The six great elements—earth, water, fire, air, space (*akasha*), and consciousness are *mahashunyata*. Usually we talk about the four great elements, but in this emptiness there are six. All the universe is moving and acting; all *samskaras*—the aggregate or *skandha* of the creative elements of your own *alaya*-consciousness—are manifesting their own elemental existence with nobody in it. When you truly understand this emptiness, you will see how all these elements come out and create the universe. No one is the master, no one is the God. They are their own action.

Buddhism is different from Christianity. There is no God in Buddhism who makes things on Monday, Tuesday, Wednesday... and on Sunday takes a rest. Who is God? If He is God, is he a

"Before-Monday" God? No one made God in Buddhism. Therefore, God is Empty; yet you can see the activity of the Universe. When you pass the koan of the banner and wind [82], when you understand this koan, you will understand non-ego, and all the creation of the world. You will actually see *mahaprajnaparamita*.

6) Reality is empty (*paramartha-shunyata*). *Paramartha* is the highest spiritual knowledge. When you attain nirvana, you attain it. The Hinayanist thinks nirvana is annihilation, that all is empty. You, however, must annihilate that idea of emptiness. All is empty, but emptiness is your conception, which is something. Therefore, destroy this conception. Then you will see Reality.

What is Reality? Outside of this phenomenal world there is no Reality, so Reality must be in this phenomenal world. There is no Reality outside of my incense bowl. In this Reality I am holding the incense bowl, but nothing looks like Reality. If you are a Zen student, you must prove this. Is Reality empty? You are asking me a question. All phenomena are Reality [strikes bowl]. It is the so-called highest knowledge when you understand that all phenomena are Reality. In the *Heart Sutra*[83] there is a famous line: "*Rupa* is *shunyata*, *shunyata* is *rupa*." *Rupa* is Emptiness, Emptiness is *rupa*. This is the keynote of Buddhism. Max Muller [84] read this sutra and was much disappointed: "All these people think this sutra is wonderful, but how stupid." The great Max Muller! I wish I had been a contemporary of his. Perhaps I could have said something to him.

7) Creative purpose is empty (*samskrita-shunyata*). The literal meaning of *samskrita* is "to put together" — "doing" in common parlance. Accordingly, doing is empty. Whatever you do, philosophically, comes to a conclusion. This is empty.

Nagarjuna [85], a famous Indian philosopher, explained emptiness very carefully in his commentaries. I wish I could translate his writings into English, but it would be a tremendous task. However, I shall speak a little on his thought.

Nagarjuna talks about why doing is empty. There are basically two answers. First, in doing, ego and the position of ego do not exist—

nothing whatever is permanent in this doing; therefore, it is empty. Second, the law of doing is ungraspable, unattainable, so doing is empty. (A Buddhist commentary is always just a short note. You must use your brain to solve the question.)

In this doing, ego and the position of ego do not exist. When you do something, who is doing it? Of course, you think you are doing it. Philosophers think about this. If you didn't eat, you couldn't do it. If you didn't sleep, you couldn't do it. If you were not born, you couldn't do it. So, after all, this doing is not you. If you do not digest your food; who does? You would perhaps say "Mr. Nature digests my food." Then who is this Mr. Nature? Is He the Son of God? Then He must be Christ. Who is God? No one knows—God knows! So doing is not *your* doing. It is very clear. You are looking at something, but *you* are not looking at anything—something without a name is looking at this.

It is very strange when you come to this place. You can immediately get into the swamp of religion if you think about it. *Who* is looking at that light? You cannot make any answer. In Buddhism when one talks about soul, one talks also about the position and place of soul. Subject and object are always expressed at the same time. So the Buddhist tries to catch this nature. Electricity [pointing to an electric light] comes into this globe, so the globe is the position of electricity. Without the globe, electricity would not be here; without the electricity, the globe would not be lit. Take the position away: can you prove electricity? Position and that which is in that position are really inseparable—both are empty, and both do not exist.

The law of doing is ungraspable. For example, we are always talking about the law—you shall not drink wine, it's bad. So America made the Prohibition law. Then, it was that wine is bad, but you can drink beer. Now you can drink anything. Laws have been made and abolished from time immemorial, so you can't make any substantial law to rule human life for two or three thousand years. There is nothing substantial in the law.

Or, we see the moon now far away. But in a million years the moon may scrape the surface of the earth, and shower debris—then all the laws of the solar system will change. Our life is so short that we cannot see the mutability of the law of the universe. There is no fixed law in the universe. What is law? In its intrinsic nature, it is ungraspable. This tells us the law of the universe has no ego, that no God made this law and rules the universe with a purpose. Since, according to Buddhist doctrines, there is no fixed plan or purpose in the creation of the universe, creative purpose is empty.

To see, hear, smell, taste, and touch are all doing. But *I* am not doing anything. The twelve *nidanas*—the twelve links in the chain of causation—are also *samskrita*. All the shadowy worlds of perception, the inner scale of consciousness, are included in this *samskrita*. Doing, seeing, hearing are also not ego, so they are empty. The whole universe is mutable; nothing is fixed or stays to form a permanent appearance. All Nature is but clouds in the sky, changeable, without substantial ego—empty.

8) Purposelessness is empty (*asamskrita-shunyata*). I translate *asamskrita* as "purposelessness." This part is stiff for beginners, but it is real Buddhism and very important.

*Asamskrita* is always negative. Literally, it would be "not prepared" or "not established for any purpose, for doing anything." Nagarjuna's commentary on this is that one attains Reality and liberates himself from being born, existing, and perishing. Anyone who attains Reality comprehends this emancipation and is liberated from life and death—that is, being born, existing, and perishing, the three phases of phenomenal existence, the law of all phenomena in the universe. But one who attains Reality liberates himself from this. When one attains Reality, one experiences freedom from the three phases of phenomenal existence and proves nirvana by that experience. So *asamskrita* is empty. (I like Nagarjuna very much. His theory is so crispy, like eating Japanese rice cakes.) So in the Dharma (Law of Reality), there is no graspable appearance of purposelessness; purposelessness is empty.

One talks of Reality, but in Reality one cannot grasp purposelessness. (This is terribly high-blown Buddhism. It's almost impossible to explain this unless you take *sanzen*.) In *sanzen* Reality is the first thing. Those who take *sanzen* will understand this. Reality is boundless, timeless, immeasurable—no shape to grasp, no color to perceive—but it exists from the beginning to the end of the universe. One who attains Reality—that is, really, your intrinsic nature—liberates himself from the three phases of external law. In short, if you attain *dharmakaya* you are not bothered by the law of *nirmanakaya*. In *nirmanakaya*, Mr. Smith takes wine, Mr. Jones doesn't. In *dharmakaya* law, Mr. Smith takes wine, Mr. Jones gets drunk. Queer, isn't it? When you send a telegram, the telegram must go through the wire from America to Japan. But if you broadcast by radio, it will spread in waves in all directions.

In Reality—in this moment [strikes gong]—there are one million years, and one million years doesn't exist. In Reality you are eating, drinking, and breathing, yet you have not been born, you do not exist—philosophically, that is. Of course, in that Reality you can free yourself from being born, existing, and perishing—and in the freeing, you understand what nirvana is, not only understand, but realize it.

*Dharmakaya* is purposelessness, but you cannot grasp it. If there is a bit of purposelessness in it, it is not *dharmakaya*, it is only a notion of *dharmakaya*. I was in purposelessness for six years, and one day I said: "This is just a notion," and I got out of it. True purposelessness is empty.

9) The conclusion is empty (*atyanta-shunyata*). *Atyanta* means in Sanskrit "limit," "long-end," but I translate it as "the conclusion."

Why is the conclusion empty? It is empty because doing is empty. Deny doing is empty, and it will carry you to purposelessness. Deny this purposelessness, this inactivity of *dharmakaya*, and it takes everything from you. Take your last penny away, and you feel poor, but you are still rich, for you have poverty. Take that poverty away, and what do you have? The conclusion is empty. This is the place for the monk. He is neither rich nor poor; he is in the conclusion of human life.

10) The beginningless is empty (*anavaragra-shunyata*). First, you must realize that there is no beginning to the universe. Nor is there

any end. If the universe had a beginning, it must also have an end, but, since there is no beginning, there is no end. When we say "beginingless," we think it means there is nothing, that zero does not produce a one, so there is nothing. Then, naturally, we begin to doubt. What is this all about? [Strikes his gong] There must be something. It had to begin somewhere. That is the logical conclusion. It is beginningless, but we cannot talk about it, for if we say it is beginningless, then logically there is nothing. It is beginingless, but everything is existing, so we cannot talk about it; we cannot make a conception of the beginningless. That is why we say the beginningless is empty. When you pass the koan, "Before mother and father, what is your original appearance?" you will realize this. Before father and mother there is nothing, but this nothing is not zero; it is something. However, as you cannot grasp that something, the beginningless is empty.

11) Undoing phenomena is empty (*anavakara-shunyata*). How do you undo phenomena? You see yellow, red, white, and blue, then you undo this, and you find noumena. Yellow, red, white, and blue are wave lengths of ether; all phenomena are nothing but the vibration of original substance. We cannot conceive of what this original substance is, so it is empty. This is the so-called "undoing of phenomena." This is your brain's work. You have a microscope—"Oh yes!" you say, "This is a wavelength of ether." You remove it, but the object remains—you undo it, but you do not destroy anything by undoing it. So undoing is empty. You undo all phenomena in the koan, "Throughout the three worlds there is nothing," but everything is still existing. By your philosophy you undo, but you cannot destroy anything. So undoing is just like your hunting a drop of water in a glass of water. You take out one drop, two drops, three drops, but you cannot destroy water. This is undoing.

12) Your own nature is empty (*prakrti-shunyata*). Hot water is hot; this is its own nature. If it is not hot, it is not hot water. The heat is not innate nature, but comes by the combination of water and heat. When the heat is gone, it is no longer hot. When you touch your body, your body is warm, but this warmth is not your real nature; it

comes by the combination of the six great elements—earth, fire, air, water, *akasha*, and consciousness. All these elements combine and then give you your nature. If there were no air, water, or fire, there would be no earth. This earth is not its own, perpetual nature. Water has its liquid nature, but if there are were no other great elements combining with it, there would be no water—liquidity is not its own nature. And air has the elements fire, water, earth. Today scientists call these by other names—carbon, oxygen, hydrogen, and so forth. All combine to create air. It is all a combination.

13) All existence is empty (*laksana-shunyata*). You have two appearances—individual and general. Your general appearance is two eyes, two ears, one nose, and so forth, and your individual appearance is beauty, ugliness, tallness, shortness, and the like. But both are like clouds in the sky; they draw existence for a while and then they disappear, so they are empty. The nature of monks observing commandments and the appearance of monks—the robed and shaved head—is just for a while. As Nature, there are the five *skandhas*. As appearance there are the six *ayatanas*, the five senses that are external and the one that is internal.

14) One's own appearance is empty (*sarvadharma-shunyata*). When you realize the emptiness of this so-called world, *sarvadharma*, you come into this part and associate with each other with compassion, separate in appearance—woman, man, father, child—repeating an old relation in karma. It is as ephemeral as lightning, appearing for such a little while. All that we can see with our eyes, and all that we can think with our brain is the result of our eye and our brain. Originally there was just a tower of emptiness, solid consciousness, of course, but no you or me—all one. Beginning and end are the same, doing and undoing are the same in that state. It is the real foundation of our soul, but, deluded by our vision, we see each other. Originally, we were one. Then, just as a finger touches another finger—"Oh, there is another finger." But there is still just one man. For a little while these figures come out into the air and sunlight, and we see each other, and love each other, but it is just a little dream.

When we confront that eternal emptiness as bodhisattvas, we naturally join hands and kneel down to it, but it is not out of fear. You must understand this with your *prajnaparamita*. Kneel down and join hands to it, concentrate your mind to it. You can see both sides; you are standing between two different existences. You are *prajna*, and you know that the two appearances are empty. This is not brain, this feeling is not philosophy. In your heart you slowly find that you are a Buddhist.

15) The ungraspable is empty (*anupalambha-shunyata*). *Samsara*, nirvana, and *sarvadharma* are ungraspable. *Samsara* is all existence on the outside, like the wheel of a cart turning endlessly. Nirvana is the extinction of this turning wheel. *Sarvadharma* is all-existence. When you open your eye you will see all-existence. In the morning someone is born, in the evening someone dies. We think fifty or seventy years is a long time, but compared with eternity it is a moment. So *samsara* is between birth and death. Nirvana is the other side of the coin. There is an interval between the time when you die in agony, and the time when you are born again; this interval is nirvana. In Buddhism "*Ahhhhh*" is the sound of birth and "*Mmmmm*" is the sound of death. On "*Ahhhhh*" all the universe appears; on "*Mmmmm*" all the universe disappears. Between "*Ahhhhh*" and "*Mmmmm*" is *samsara*; between "*Mmmmm*" and "*Ahhhhh*" is nirvana.

To understand nirvana you do not need to die. You can understand it immediately, here and now. You do not need to close your eyes, or stop your mind movement. When your eye is open and you are thinking something, nirvana exists in the back of your consciousness. You should know about it, that is all. If you have ten dollars in your pocket, you don't need to take it out and count it. You just know it is there. You have nirvana in the pocket of your consciousness. Don't put off thinking about it until the moment of your death.

*Samsara* and nirvana are really everything. *Samsara* is something and nirvana is nothing, but this nothing is something and this something is nothing. Also, something is something, and nothing is nothing, and both are empty. Understood this way, *samsara* and nirvana are ungraspable.

So you cannot find your self inside the five *skandhas*. In all existing appearances, perceptions, subconscious, thoughts, and consciousness and the outside, which consists of the great elements, there is no separate ego. You cannot find your self in water, in fire, in air—anywhere—so you cannot find your self outside yourself.

You cannot find your self in your physical body (*rupa*). You think your body is your self, but your body is also made up of the great elements; so you cannot find your self in your physical body.

Thoughts (*samjna*) are not your self. They are impressions from the outside. Since you cannot find your self outside, obviously you cannot find your self in the impressions of the outside.

The subconscious (*samskara*) consists of subliminal mind movement. A Western scholar translates *samskara* as "accumulation of the creative faculty"—feeling and emotion, moods in Nature. When you see this outside it is all the emotions depicted by Nature in the phenomenal world. The willow weeps, the pine tree laughs, the tiger is ferocious, the dog woofs, the cat meows. This creative faculty is really the seed of all existence. In this *samskara* you cannot find your self; it is nothing but the vibration of your consciousness. It changes like ripples of water. If you have a good feeling, the ripples are smooth; and if you have an angry feeling, there are big waves.

Consciousness digests your food, awakes and sleeps, and you have nothing to do with it. You have no power over it; it is not yours, for consciousness is not your self, and you cannot find your self in it. Therefore, it is ungraspable.

As for the twelve gates or entrances (*ayatana*), we can explain how they are ungraspable as we did with the five *skandhas*. You cannot find your self in the sense gates—the eyes, ears, nose, pores, and so forth—any more than you can find your fist in your five fingers.

If you try to find why you seek Dharma, you also cannot find any substantial reason as well. Are you afraid of death? Your consciousness dies, but you do not. Your consciousness is not your self. Do you seek Dharma because you want to understand? There is nothing to understand, for all the outside, all the inside is nothing, so you are wasting your energy. You cannot find any reason why you search for religion, but you have to search for it. You are looking for something to grasp in relative existence. When you realize there is no substantial Reality in existence, you are afraid you cannot grasp Reality. This fear is empty. You do not need to have this fear, and when you realize there is nothing to grasp, then you have grasped it. This conception of the ungraspable is also empty.

16) Non-existence is empty (*abhavashvabha-shunyata*). When all *dharmas* cease to exist at the end of the universal fire, and all has been reduced to nothing, it is "no-*dharma*." But is it really no-*dharma*? For from that emptiness the new universe will be created. So non-being is empty. (*Abhava* is here translated "non-existence." In Sanskrit *a* is a negative prefix; *bhava* is "to be, to exist.")

17) Existence is empty (*bhava-shunyata*). All dharmas exist in accordance with the law of causality, but existence is not really existing, so it is empty. If we really understand the emptinesses, *shunyatas*, these phenomena, *dharmas*, cease to exist.

18) Non-existing existence is empty (*abhava-shunyata*). First we must understand that all objective existences are empty. Next we must think of these two existences (non-existence and existence) as empty. Both are your notions, your subjective attitudes, and attitudes are empty. So what does "non-existing existence is empty" mean? One who is tenacious of either of the two conceptions cannot find the reality of them. Therefore we call them empty. First we deny the existence we adhere to and second we deny the conception we adhere to in denying it.

Thus all eighteen *shunyatas* are empty, so you do not need to think any more. You simply have to return here [points to his heart]. "Yes" is empty; "no" is empty. "Yes-and-no" is empty; "no-and-yes" is empty. This is the conclusion of philosophic Buddhism, and the starting point of Zen. So when you practice meditation, sit down, cross your legs, fold your hands, and clear up your mind, you enter into the Great Universe, and the Great Universe enters into you. There is no distinction between you and the Great Universe—you are one. Thoughts vanish from your mind, and you enter into boundless existence. It is the beginning of Zen; it is not yourself. From that truth you will emerge as THAT—Tathagata—the one who comes exactly as THAT.

# THE FOUR WISDOMS

W hen you attain the highest wisdom, your consciousness becomes Wisdom-Itself. The consciousness that was previously in the state of leakage (discharging interior disturbances through the five *skandhas*, much as you perspire through the pores of your skin) turns into Wisdom—the All-Wisdom of Buddha

The secret of enlightenment is this hairpin turn, as I always call it. It is like a turn in the road. It's as if you were to enter the North Star [zenith], turn yourself to the south [nadir], and control the zodiac at once. If you don't understand this hairpin turn, you don't understand Buddhism.

The Four Wisdoms (*jnana*) together are the Buddha's wisdom. The Buddha's wisdom has these four natures:

1) Mirrorlike Wisdom (*adarsha-jnana*)—the wisdom that is like a perfect mirror; it perceives the outside and inside together in oneness [86].

2) Undiscerning Wisdom (*samata-jnana*)—usually translated as "sameness" or "equality." With this meaning, however, it discerns sentient and insentient beings without discrimination, as the surface of a pond reflects flowers, rocks, dogs, and human beings at the same time, without making any discrimination. In another sense, *samata-jnana* may be translated as "uniform wisdom," the wisdom "common" to all sentient beings; it perceives all outside forms and existences without discrimination, without adherence to or preference for any particular appearance, including the phenomena that appear in the mind. It perceives indifferently [87]. When a donkey peeps into a well, the donkey has adherence, but the well sees the donkey without any adherence to the donkey. In the same way, the second

wisdom observes all states, all phases of appearance. In activity, it is the activity of observation and introspection, the third wisdom.

3) Observing Wisdom (*pratyaveksana-jnana*)—the activity of observing the phenomena that appear on the inside, in the mind, and that which appears on the outside. Observation of the inside is "introspective wisdom"; observation of the outside is "perspective wisdom." With the third wisdom, the Buddha observes every detail of existence.

4) Performing Wisdom (*krityanusthana-jnana*)—the performance of the Buddha in action.

Thus, Wisdom has four natures and four corresponding consciousnesses. The first wisdom, Mirrorlike Wisdom, is immobile, like earth. The other three wisdoms depend upon it. It corresponds to the eighth consciousness, the *alayavijnana*. The *alaya* is in the state of leakage, but when it is enlightened, it becomes Mirrorlike Wisdom, the Tathagata's virtue, possessed in body (*buddhakaya*) and dominion (*buddhakshetra*), the mirror consciousness. Everything is perceived on this mirror infinitely through time and space.

The seventh consciousness (*manovijnana*) is in the state of leakage also. When it is enlightened, it becomes Undiscerning Wisdom. The sixth consciousness, this present consciousness, is *klista-manas*. It corresponds to Observing Wisdom; it observes the differentiation of inside and outside existence. The fifth consciousness corresponds to the five senses; it is Performing Wisdom.

When you attain Undiscerning Wisdom, you realize you have no ego; you attain the awareness that your consciousness is not an ego but the consciousness common to all sentient beings. With this understanding you awaken to Great Compassion. Great Compassion means you perform without partiality.

When you attain Observing Wisdom, eradicate others' mortifications and destroy others' doubts. You observe existence in each sense-perception and in each successive stage of consciousness. You have knowledge with which to reach emancipation from doubt and mortification.

With Performing Wisdom, you promulgate the Buddha's teachings and convert the people in the stages of *shravaka* and *pratyeka-buddha*. With bodhisattvas, you do not use tricks or devices (*upayas*) [88]. But to those sentient beings who have no bodhisattva nature, you do, such as building beautiful temples, playing lovely music, painting wonderful frescoes, using various terms in philosophy, etc. With laymen you use business—buying and selling, giving and receiving. Sentient beings, not only the Buddha, have these four wisdoms when they are enlightened.

In the Shingon sect of Buddhism, there is added one more wisdom—Pure Wisdom, the wisdom of the pure nature of the entire universe (*dharmadhatu-prakrti-jnana*). This pure wisdom corresponds to the *amalavijnana*, the ninth consciousness. *Alaya*-consciousness is sentient consciousness; *amala*-consciousness is insentient consciousness—earth, fire, water, and so forth, have this pure consciousness, which carries no seed of karma; thus they count five.

Pure Wisdom corresponds to the ether, space. Mirrorlike Wisdom corresponds to earth. Undiscerning Wisdom corresponds to fire, as it consumes everything into its own wisdom. Observing Consciousness corresponds to water, and Performing Consciousness corresponds to air; as it moves, it shakes everything on earth.

Corresponding to each of the five wisdoms are five Buddhas:

1. Pure Wisdom—Vairochana Buddha, the Great Sun Buddha of the Center.

2. Mirrorlike Wisdom—Aksobhya Buddha, the Buddha of the Eastern Sky, the beginning of all movement.

3. Undiscerning Wisdom—Ratnasambhava Buddha, the Buddha of the Southern Sky, the Buddha of productive power, the Buddha who produces jewels.

4. Observing Wisdom—Amitabha Buddha, the Buddha of Western Sky, the Setting Sun, the Buddha of Everlasting Age. In the light of the setting sun, everything becomes bright and clear, as the Buddha observes.

5. Performing Wisdom—Shakyamuni Buddha, the Buddha of the Northern Sky. In the Shingon sect he is named Amoghasiddhi Buddha.

Vairochana Buddha is at the center, and at the four corners— East, West, North, and South—are the other Buddhas manifesting their Wisdom [89].

# THE TRIUNE BODY OF BUDDHA

The three bodies of Buddha, the *trikaya* in Sanskrit, is the triune body of Buddha. They are not three different bodies but three aspects of the one body of Buddha. The first body is *dharmakaya*, the second is *sambhogakaya*, and the third is *nirmanakaya*, *kaya* being the word for "body."

To describe the relationship between these bodies, a moon metaphor is frequently used in which *dharmakaya* is the body of the moon, *sambhogakaya* is the light of the moon, and *nirmanakaya* is the reflection of the moon on water. The *trikaya* is a profound doctrine, analogous to the Trinity in Christianity, and as it is difficult to understand, I am not eager to speak about it.

*Sambhogakaya* has been translated as "enjoyment," and *sambhogakaya* as the "body of enjoyment," but we cannot translate it this way. The "body of unity," or "body of yoga" would be a better translation, because *sambhogakaya* stands between all outside, or phenomena, and all inside, or noumena. Of course, I do not mean that phenomena are only outside and noumena only inside, but I speak about them as outside and inside for convenience.

There is a metaphor found in old Indian Buddhism of a mirror in the sky. When the mirror hangs in the sky, nothing is reflected on its surface. If it fails to perform its function—to be conscious of its own existence—it disappears. For without outside there is no inside, neither is there anything between outside and inside. The consciousness referred to as the mirror is between the outside and the inside, like the hinge of a door or the link of a chain connecting two entities. Therefore, it is called the *sambhogakaya*, the body that joins two sides.

When you listen to a Buddhist sermon, you must realize that you are listening to something about yourself. I am not talking about something that is in the sky; I am talking about your own consciousness, you own mind, the mind that is clear as crystal, your consciousness of yourself. Buddhists are not talking about something remote, but about something very close to you. For the Buddhist, God is not living far away; the Buddhist God is living in your own mind.

*Sambhogakaya* functions in two ways. The first way is toward others; the second is toward itself. "Toward others" is to see the outside—mountains, rivers, lakes, cities, farms, and villages, men and women, and all animal life. It is also to be conscious of varying conditions. today, I feel very hot, so I take off my coat. Today I feel very cold, so I put on my coat. Now I am sleepy, so I sleep, and so on. The *sambhogakaya* function toward itself is to introspect its own existence, to meditate upon its own existence, as I meditate upon my own mind.

When I came to this country, I found that there was a Christian sect called Quakers and that these Quakers meditate upon themselves and empty their minds in order to receive the revelation of God. When your mind is filled up with something, it cannot receive the revelation of God. So they empty their minds in order that the revelation of God may flash through it. This is something like Buddhism. But I observed that often, when they stood up and talked, what they said had little inspiration. They ought always to wait for real inspiration; then they could speak.

The Buddhist way is to meditate upon oneself and to penetrate to the depths of one's own consciousness, and this consciousness is like a mirror that has two surfaces, one toward the outside, and one toward the bottomless inside. On the surface that is toward the outside, there are many reflections—mountains and rivers, men and women. On the surface to the inside there are no reflections; only infinite Emptiness is reflected. But this infinite Emptiness is not empty; it possesses omnipotent power. Emptiness, in Buddhism, is not empty like an empty bottle; it is filled up solid. But this solid inside is pure, uniform, and immobile, so that it looks empty. When you mistake this Emptiness for emptiness, you fall into agnosticism and nihilism. It is not void emptiness; it is solid emptiness.

*Sambhogakaya* is your present consciousness. You are aware of it. You have it now. *Sambhogakaya* is axiomatic; it proves its own truth by itself. Without any debate, without any demonstration, you can believe in your own consciousness, your own awareness. Awareness-itself is God in Buddhism. We call it Buddha. Gautama attained the highest awareness; therefore, we call him Buddha. The God of Buddhism is very plain. This awareness which I have and you have is uniform. It comes from the same source, so we see the same forms, the same colors, etc.

This present consciousness is *sambhogakaya*, so do not think I am talking of something else. I am talking about the consciousness that is burning incense, speaking to you, drinking water. Western people call it "I." We don't call it I. We don't need an I. It is *sambhogakaya*. It is Buddha's second body.

Then what is the first body? The first body is bottomless Emptiness. IT is omnipresent, it fills the universe. IT fills time—past, present, and future. IT is pure; there is nothing to IT. IT is pure time and space. So Buddha does not feel time and space in IT—there is no time and space. IT is His wisdom, His omnipotent power. But there is no way of looking at it from the human side. IT is the first body—*dharmakaya*.

The consciousness that appears in a person and performs and works in daily life is called *nirmanakaya*, the "body of transforma-tion"—that is, transformation into the bodies of birds and beasts, fire and air; transformation into the bodies of butchers, fishmongers, emperors, presidents, soldiers. It transforms its body into all occupa-tions and all instruments. This body of transformation, is symbolized by the image of the Bodhisattva Avalokiteshvara. He has a thousand hands holding a thousand instruments, and in the tip of each finger, there is an eye—Thousand-eyed Avalokiteshvara, or in Chinese, Kuan-yin.

*Sambhogakaya* is symbolized by the image of the bodhisattva Samantabhadra, the bodhisattva of universal virture. Samantabhadra sits on the back of a huge white elephant that has six tusks. The six tusks represent the six consciousnesses of eye, ear, nose, tongue, skin, and mind. The whiteness of the elephant symbolizes uniformity. Samantabhadra is neither man nor woman, and has a very naive face.

*Dharmakaya* is always symbolized by a child, by Bodhisattva Manjushri in a child's form, because the child does not yet realize his conscious existence.

I don't like to talk of Buddhism in Christian terms, but sometimes there are analogies between the two religions. The three bodies of Buddha may be likened to the Trinity in Christianity. *Nirmanakaya* is the equivalent of Jesus; *sambhogakaya* the equivalent of the Holy Ghost, the Christ Spirit; and *dharmakaya* the equivalent of God.

# AWAKENING

A wakening is important term in Buddhism, because Buddhism itself rests upon it—upon the awakening of wisdom, the awakening not of the brain center but of the wisdom center. What wisdom actually is, and what the center of man's cognition is, are great problems for both philosophers and religious men. Of course, awakening is easy to talk about—but the awakening of what? I awake from sleep, but awakening for the Buddhist is not from physical sleep.

The Buddha taught that the first awakening is initial awakening, the beginning of awakening. By it one awakes to the fact that he was sleeping and is now awake; that is, he was unaware of his existence, unaware of his awakened consciousness. This is easy to understand. Before awakening you are not aware of sleep, but in the morning you realize that you have been asleep. In a spiritual awakening—a handy phrase!—you realize you were unaware of sleeping; you have been in sleeping consciousness, even though you eat and drink and work. With initial awakening, you realize your consciousness was asleep. A man who has lived in awakened consciousness, however, cannot go back to sleep. The famous Chinese Zen poet, Kanzan ("Cold Mountain")[90], wrote:

> *I have been living ten years upon Kanzan*
> *The top is so steep and high*
> *Shrouded by white clouds*
> *Even the birds cannot trace*
> *The sharp rise of the peak*

Occasionally, he came down to the foot of the mountain to visit his temple friends. (I think you will recall a famous picture in China or Japan of two hermits in black robes, standing in front of a little fire of autumn leaves, smiling happily and talking.)

Kanzan was saying that for ten years he could not go back to the foot of the mountain. He had lost his way down because he had been living on the peak. The clouds, shrouding the rocks that soar into the sky, closed off the entire range from all birds. "Birds" means the birds in the mind, singing from morning to evening without stop. His wisdom—his spiritual body—is living on that high mountain peak, and no birds—no whisper of the brain— can reach there. When I go to Second or Third Avenue on 59th Street, with the El-train running, the clamor fills the air, and I cannot hear my own mind. But Kanzan could not hear his mind even when it was whispering.

This is a nicely expressed poem by a hermit, though it does not express the core of Buddhism. Kanzan was in the awakened stage and could not go back any more. When you enter the awakened condition, you realize that you have been sleeping. If you think of this sleeping condition and this awakened condition, you will understand that there are three consciousnesses—the intrinsic consciousness, awakened consciousness, and sleeping consciousness. And so we realize that our awakened consciousness is the intrinsic consciousness. It is within you, latent; one day you will awake suddenly, and you will realize—"This is what I've been looking for so many, many years! Now I've come close to it, and I realize that IT is myself—my world, my universe! And this is my home!"

From that day on you do not need to search around for anything anymore. There is nothing to search for. "Well, I have finally awakened after *kalpas* of reincarnations, and it was within me. Now I have suddenly awakened, and this is the answer."For about two or three days you will feel that you are standing in mid-air, and after four or five months you will realize that you are living in THAT— eating THAT, drinking THAT, just THAT—the Tathagata. IT comes exactly as THAT.

I have explained the circumstances and atmosphere of awakening, but I have not yet talked about the real point of awakening. What is it, really? One cannot speak about it—there is nothing to say—

one's tongue is too short to say anything about it—words limit meaning. So in Zen, or any other sect of Buddhism, teachers try to hand this point to you without words. You must realize this body is THAT—mind and wisdom and all this universe is THAT, not matter or spirit, but THAT. In Sanskrit, *bhutatathata*, in English, "Isness." You will need to open your eyes wider or look up to the sky or kneel upon the floor. THIS IS THAT! Some day, in some corner of your mind, it will come. "My Son, thou art always with me."

In the Shingon school the priests will ask you to concentrate on the letter, "A." "A" has the shape of wings, sky, emptiness. You imagine that there is a big moon. You place this "A" in your abdomen, in the center of the moon, and meditate upon it. The sun shines into the moon, and the moon shines back into the sun, and suddenly, someday—Ah!—THIS IS THAT! That is the beginning. Then you will not need the moon, the sun, and "A" any more. "A" was beginningless, and "A" will be endless. I am IT. In the Zen school if you say "A" the priest says, "Shut your mouth, and throw it away! Sit down with nothing!" The Shingon monk uses "A" like a cane. He says within this "A" we sleep and eat. The Zen monk says, "Within or without—nothing." When you really awaken you have nothing to talk about. That is the beginning. You are initiated.

When I came here everybody talked about "initiation." Some teachers collected twenty-five dollars for it. But though you pile up one thousand dollars you cannot purchase awakening. It has nothing to do with initiation. Initiation into what? Since I have not much courage to speak of the heart of Buddhism, I have strayed from the real point. Perhaps you do not understand yet.

The Buddha made the metaphor of the mirror, of the mirror in the pure sky. This sky is not the space that our sight and eye perceives, though that does give us an idea of the infinite. Einstein said that the universe is finite but boundless. Our life has beginning and end; it is finite, but it is also infinite and limitless. Certainly he made a wonderful remark. The world has end and beginning, of course, from *kalpa* to *kalpa*; yet, it is boundless.

The Buddha also speaks of no time and no space, where if I make a sound there is in that single moment a million years. It is spaceless like radio waves, like electric space—intrinsic. The Buddha said that there is a mirror that reflects consciousness. In this electric space a million miles and a pinpoint—a million years and a moment—are exactly the same. It is pure essence. Modern science might call it a quantum, or an electron, or proton. (The quantum is perhaps not pure essence, but one can call it so.) Matter and spirit are the same in that space. There is a mirror but nothing reflects upon it. We call it "original consciousness"—"original *akasha*"—perhaps God in the Christian sense. I am afraid of speaking about anything that is not familiar to me. No one can know what IT is.

Fire is burning. What is that which is burning? If there is no air, no wood, or no match, no fire will burn. So what is fire really? Edison said he did not know what electricity is.

The Buddha said, IT has eyes, ears, nose, mouth—everything. IT has Law in its manifestation, essential Law in its constitution. You can see it in crystallization. You can see it in a tree. The human body also has the shape of a tree. Everything that has the nature of essential consciousness takes its own shape, its own crystallization. We call it the first law, *dharmakaya*. But we cannot speak of the first law. The second law is the explosion, *sambhogakaya*. When this comes to our mind we find entire freedom of mind. All is symmetrical. How does it grow distorted? The third law is a one-way road, *nirmanakaya*. Even though we have had the fourth dimensional explosion in our realization, in our daily life we must take the one-way road.

# THE BUDDHA'S SILENCE

T *hus have I heard:*

*Once the Buddha was sojourning in Karanda-Venuvana in Rajagriha. Mahakashyapa and Shariputra were sojourning upon Mount Gridhrakuta. At that time there were many heretic monks. One day some of them visited Shariputra. When they met Shariputra they saluted him and inquired about his health. Then they withdrew to one side and, having seated themselves, put the following questions to him:*

*"How think you Shariputra, will Tathagata have life-and-death in the future?"*

*Shariputra answered the heretic monks: "Lokanatha's* [91] *answer on this point was, 'Silence.'"* [92]

*The monks questioned again: "How think you Shariputra, will Tathagata have no life-and-death in the future?"*

*Shariputra answered the heretic monks: "The Buddha answered, 'Silence.'"*

*Again they asked Shariputra: "Will Tathagata both have life-and-death and no life-and-death in the future?"*

*Shariputra replied to them: "On this point Lokanatha answered, 'Silence.'"*

*Again they questioned: "Shariputra, will Tathagata have neither life-and-death nor no life-and-death in the future?"*

*Shariputra answered the heretic monks: "Lokanatha answered, 'Silence.'"*

*Once more the heretic monks questioned Shariputra: "To those questions that were put to the Tathagata—will*

*Tathagata have life-and-death in the future, or will he have no life-and-death in the future, or will he have both life-and-death and no life-and-death in the future, or will he have neither life-and-death nor no life-and-death in the future—to all those questions why was Lokanatha's answer 'Silence'? It is like an idiot's or a fool's answer. It decides nothing, it explains nothing. He is like an infant; he has no self-knowledge."*

*Thus they spoke. Then they rose from their seats and departed.*

In the early sutras there are many descriptions of the answer made by the Buddha to questions about his future life and death. Some heretic monks asked the Buddha this question directly. The Buddha's answer was SILENCE, in Sanskrit, *avyakrita.* Temporarily I translate this word as "no-word"—literally, "said nothing." But it is not sufficient to say he remained silent, and to translate his answer as "silence." To adopt his silent attitude is not to remain silent, because his attitude of silence is not *mere* silence.

The Chinese used a word to express the Buddha's SILENCE—"mute thunder." Such an important principle of Buddhism cannot be explained with words. Of course, there are many words with which it is talked about—*akasha, shunyata,* emptiness, etc. When you look at a glass of water, there is nothing in it, so it is empty—but it is solid emptiness. Of course, you can use a Buddhist term like "*dharmakaya.*" And you can say Buddha's *dharmakaya* is omnipresent, omnipotent, omniscient; or you can apply a Western philosophical term such as "reality," or "absolute nothingness."

In the beginning, when I was giving lectures here in New York, when I sat in SILENCE the audience thought the Reverend has forgotten a word and is sitting thinking about it. But it is not that. My meaning was that there were no words to speak about it with. Then some of my audience would say, "Reverend, do you need a dictionary?"

No, I don't need a dictionary. This is not written in a dictionary. The human being cannot explain THIS. I said THIS; I didn't say "this attitude" or "this silence." I said THIS. Human beings cannot explain THIS.

In Sanskrit this attitude or state is called *tatha*—"nothing but this, or that." You cannot explain it with words. It is the absolute truth of the state of Reality. It is undemonstrable. It is unintelligible. The human intellect fails to intellectualize it. You might say, "God has no name." But there is an accurate word to express THIS, an absolute word to convey its meaning. This word is SILENCE.

This word covers all the universe and penetrates from the beginningless beginning to the endless end. And it is an existence. Throughout the universe this silence is nothing but TATHA existing. In your words, "God."

However, the universe was not created by someone; the universe is an existence from the beginningless beginning to the endless end. The Buddha came from there and returns there. Therefore, we call him Tathagata. *Gata* means "come." He has come from nowhere, and will go nowhere. Thus He has come, and thus He will go. He came to earth, transfiguring himself into human shape with two legs, exactly as THAT.

It is foolish to ask a question like, "Has Tathagata a future life?"

SILENCE.

"Has He no future life?"

SILENCE.

Shariputra's answer to the heretic monks, *avyakrita*, is accurate and clear. If the heretic monks' eyes could see this solid emptiness, they would understand this answer without saying a word. There is no need to say yes or no. This is the very pivot of Buddhism. Of course, if we want to describe this answer on paper, we cannot just leave an empty space, so we use a word like *avyakrita*. When you record notes of music the blank space is *avyakrita*. *Avyakrita* is a word, but it is used here as the symbol of SILENCE.

That is the outline of the sutra.

The heretic monks were disappointed, however. *It is like an idiot's or a fool's answer. It explains nothing. He is like an infant; he has no self-knowledge.* Thus they spoke. Then they rose from their seats and departed. Pigs don't understand the value of a diamond. Shariputra made a wonderful answer. His speech was loud as thunder, but deaf-mutes could not hear a word of what he said. In another sutra, this type of teaching takes a different turn.

The Buddha was meditating on the roadside. A thunderbolt struck a huge tree, split the tree in half, and killed nine oxen. A pedestrian found the Buddha on the roadside meditating.

"O Buddha, did you hear that terrific thunder?"

The Buddha answered, "No."

"Your meditation was so profound you did not hear the thunder? The thunderbolt crashed through a great tree and split the tree in two. Didn't you hear the crash?"

The Buddha kept silent.

"It killed nine oxen. Did you know that?

"No."

The pedestrian extolled the Buddha's profound and bottomless *samadhi*: "Buddha, you are wonderful. You did not hear that terrific thunder!"

When people read this sutra they think the Buddha really did not hear the thunder. Can you understand Buddhism if you understand this sutra in such a way? How foolish! How can a human being in meditation make his present consciousness so numb that he could not hear a thunderbolt that split a tree and killed nine oxen? Such Buddhism is trash! Of course, the Buddha knew quite well the thunderbolt crashed, saw the lightning, saw the tree fall on two sides and kill nine oxen. But the Buddha observed this phenomenon from the standpoint of the essential existence of the universe, and he expressed it—there was no sound, no light, no tree; neither thunder nor oxen, neither space nor time, neither past nor present nor future. It is absolute, it is infinite.

But the Buddha did not speak in such a way. His attitude was different from that of the usual religious teacher. He simply said nothing, and his disciples described it exactly. But blind men cannot read that sutra. Their minds must be enlightened to read it.

This is one of the sutras that speaks of the profound principle that is the pivot of Buddhism, that is, as I have said, SILENCE.

What is the pivot of the teaching in Christianity? God! In Buddhism? THIS! THIS is the pivot of our teaching. Someone said, "Oh, Osho [93], don't make that funny face. I can't help but laugh when you do that." I am very sorry, but I am not making any funny face. I am only sitting here in SILENCE. There is no other way to express it. At the beginning of my lecture I always sit thus a little while. That is the beginning of my lecture.

The heretic monks did not belong to the Buddha's *sangha*. They believed in ego, believed that after death there is an ego, a soul that goes somewhere like an airplane and stays there. Buddhists do not believe in an ego. Our ego is so tremendously boundless it is the whole universe. It has no core. It is not like a peach, or an apple. This whole universe is Oneness, Consciousness, Soul, Ego. We don't need to put little egos in it like little spots—the entire universe is myself. Ego is the universe.

So the heretic monks thought: We are going to catch the Buddha. If he says that he exists after death, then we will ask him, "So where do you exist after death?" and catch him. There was a trick in this question.

The questions of the monks were in the usual form or construction of the logic of India: 1) Has he? 2) Has he not? 3) Does he both have and have not? 4) Does he neither have nor have not? European scholars often avoid all such forms, but for the Buddhist these forms must be observed.

This type of sutra is difficult to read and difficult to understand. If you just buy a book and read it, it is hard to grasp the point. You cannot grasp it. But once you have heard it explained with the Buddhist's traditional knowledge, you will not forget. You will remember always.

# THE SILENCE OF SURABHA

The Buddha's teaching is twofold. It is like going and coming back, ascending and descending. It is like rowing a boat against the current to the source of a river and, then, flowing back down toward the ocean. To study Buddhism you start from here, from this daily life. You will practice many Buddhistic contrivances; and then, you will attain nirvana. When you attain nirvana, naturally you will turn from there to this usual daily life again. You will find your own position between heaven and earth. You will really find yourself emancipated from all the usual agonies. But always there is someone who asks, "Well if we must go up only to come down again and find a place at the foot of the mountain where we will be contented, why must we go up to the top of the mountain at all? Why not remain at the foot of the mountain and avoid such useless exertion?" Many answer, "Going up the mountain is a monk's business; we laymen need not undertake such an activity."

This is a common Buddhist attitude. Many Buddhists conceive such a notion in order to become more contented with themselves. And always there is someone who says, "Whenever anyone asked the Buddha a difficult question, the Buddha answered with silence."

So he thinks silence is Zen! "In the Zen school," he says, "we are taught to be quiet, so let's keep quiet! For after all, there is nothing to say, and there will be nothing to say. So why should we strive for nothingness, and striving for it finally arrive at our original stupidity?"

Such are the answers given by half-baked Buddhists.

Once when the Buddha was sojourning at Vulture Peak, there was a young heretic named Surabha who had once been a disciple of the Buddha. He was not a young man but rather about the Buddha's age. He often said to his disciples in a loud voice, "I know all about the Buddha's Dharma. I knew all about it before I became his disciple, and now I have abandoned it all. I have abandoned the Buddha's Dharma entirely."

The Buddha's disciples, who went down to the castle in the early morning wearing their robes and holding bowls for begging food overheard what was being said by this heretic Surabha. They heard him saying that he knew all about the Buddha's Dharma, that he knew all about it before he became the Buddha's disciple, and that now he had abandoned it all.

After begging from door to door, the monks went back to the garden, finished their meal, and washed their bowls, and their feet. Coming into the presence of the Buddha, they bowed down before him, retired to their own seats, and repeated what they had heard from Surabha. They said to the Buddha, "We pray you, Tathagata, go down there and speak to him out of pity." The Buddha, accepting in silence, went down to the bank of the river where Surabha was preaching.

When the Buddha and his disciples arrived, Surabha was in the midst of talking to his disciples. He had been saying as before, "I know all about the Buddha's Dharma, knew all about it before I became his disciple, and now I have abandoned it all. I do not care anything about him. I have abandoned him. Someday I will go and give the fellow hell!" As he was talking, he saw the Buddha approaching. What a conclusion for his talk! What will he do?

The Buddha came with his disciples, came clear as the moon among the stars, and with a face calm as clear water. He came slowly to the bank of that river, and Surabha quickly spread his mat on the ground in welcome. "Pray be seated," said Surabha. He couldn't help himself. The Buddha's presence was like the direct rays of a brilliant sun. When you face such a brilliant light, you must shut your eyes. The Buddha saluted Surabha and went to the seat and sat down crosslegged.

Immediately the Buddha questioned Surabha. "Have you truly said that you knew all about my Dharma, that you had known it before you became my disciple, and now have forsaken it and do not care for my Dharma anymore? Tell me, is this true?"

Surabha bowed in silence and did not answer a word.

The Buddha said to him, "Surabha, why are you silent? Say something. If your talk is good, I shall be delighted. If your talk is imperfect, I shall make it perfect, and you will be contented with it."

Still Surabha remained silent.

Was he imitating the Buddha? Was the silence of Surabha like the silence of the Buddha when someone asked him a question and he kept silent? I will not agree with anyone who thinks it was. The silence of Surabha was the silence of cowardice.

Imagine the confusion of Surabha's disciples when they saw their teacher cowed. He could not speak a word. Among them was a young man who spoke up and said to Surabha, "My teacher, I think you should repeat what you just said to us, that you knew all about Buddhism before you became the Buddha's disciple, know all about it now, and that you do not care anything about him and have abandoned him. I think that you should speak. You are always saying that you will go to the Buddha and give him hell. Well, the Buddha came to you. Why don't you give him hell right now? Tell him all that you just told us about Shakyamuni Gautama. The Buddha said that if your opinion was good, he would be delighted, and if it was not good, he would make it perfect. Why do you hesitate to speak to him?"

But Surabha remained silent, his eyes closed and his head down. Slowly the Buddha opened his lips to speak—now he will make a lion's roar!—and said, "If anyone says that Shakyamuni Gautama is not Tathagata, that he has not attained the highest enlightenment, I will ask him the reason he has for saying so. If his conception is wrong, I shall be a good friend to him, and discuss his error with him, giving him reasons and an explanation for it." (The Buddha was a kind and loving man, but his love was not lukewarm. His compassion was like fire!)

That was the Buddha's attitude. It was a very interesting moment. You can see Zen in such a moment. Now what will happen?

Surabha's disciples do not speak a word, but they are thinking many things. The Buddha gave Surabha just a short *"Ahh"*—a lion-roar! If it had been Lin-chi, he would have given Surabha a shout—*"Kaaaaaaaa!"*

The Buddha said, "Those who are out of the orbit of the true Dharma take an attitude like your keeping quiet, Surabha."

When Surabha remained silent to the very end, the Buddha spoke no word more but started home.

After the Buddha had left, the young disciple said to Surabha, "You were like an ox whose horns have been cut, kneeling down in an empty pasture to make a big noise. You can roar in the presence of your disciples, but in the presence of a real lion you keep silence. As when a woman imitates a hero on the stage, she puts on his costumes and assumes his characteristics, but when this hero speaks it is in the voice of a woman. In front of a real lion you kept silent. Your silence is like that of a fox in a cave."

This story gives you a clear conception of the difference in the silence of the Buddha and the silence of Surabha. The sound of the silence of one who transcends this life and then returns to live it is different. It is said, "When someone goes to the summit and returns to his little village, his voice is really different."

# THE BLACK STONE GROTTO

If you go to Arizona or Nevada, you may see men living in isolated huts in the mountains or deserts. But they are not hermits, only outlaws or hobos. In India, in the Buddha's time, however, there were many who lived in the woods or stone grottos under cliffsides who were not outlaws or tramps, but thinkers. One such man was Vakkali. He was a well-bred man, a Brahmin. The grotto where he stayed was not on a mountainside, but on a very steep hill. One day Vakkali saw the Buddha passing by. The Buddha and his *sangha* were traveling from Shravasti to some other town. Vakkali was struck by the Buddha's dignity, his tranquil expression, and well-formed body. The Buddha seemed to him like the moon among the stars. When we speak about the Buddha, we often mention the thirty-two physiognomic signs that his ideal appearance revealed, the marks of his buddhahood. There is also a thirty-third sign, but this is indescribable, so it is not listed among those that are revealed on his face and body.

As the Buddha passed by Vakkali's grotto, the hermit contemplated the Buddha's wonderful appearance as in a dream. All of a sudden he realized that he must become his disciple, but it was too late, for the traveling procession had already passed the foot of the hill. Vakkali started after them, but he feared he would not overtake them. It was evening. Rushing down, feeling that he was losing the way in the dark, he flung himself down the side of the hill and fell before the Buddha. But before his feet could touch the ground, the Buddha held him up. (There are many descriptions like this in the sutras. You must read these parts as the writer's poetical touch.) It was as if his decision to become the Buddha's disciple was so overpowering, he jumped from a cliff to fall at the Buddha's feet. At the precise moment his feet touched the ground, the Buddha held his hand so he could stand up. There is an additional touch of symbolism here, too, but it is a minor point, and somewhat irrelevant, so I will not put any emphasis upon it.

Vakkali was fascinated with the statuelike modeling of the Buddha's face and his sublime expression. His eyes fixed upon him and he could not take them from his face—he had become attached to the Buddha's phenomenal appearance. Day and night he followed the Buddha, watching him as a cat watches a mouse hole, meditating and concentrating upon his appearance. It wasn't the Buddha's real appearance, of course—one cannot see the Reality of Buddha—but a fascination with the Buddha's physical appearance, just as you might become fascinated with the appearance of the actor Paul Robeson, and go back to see him in a movie many, many times [94].

The Buddha realized what Vakkali was doing and did not appreciate it. "Dreadful, always looking at my body and my face, day and night, from head to toe and toe to head." The Buddha made Vakkali leave. "Go away. I forbid you to follow me."

Vakkali was terribly disappointed. He couldn't live without looking at the Buddha's wonderful appearance. What a disciple! So he decided to commit suicide by jumping off a cliff. (It was from the Eagle-Shaped Mountain, not a very high mountain, but something like those lower California hills. It was not a very well-shaped mountain, either, but a mass of gigantic rocks.)

Perceiving with his supernatural power what Vakkali was about to do, the Buddha suddenly revealed his entire physical body to him. Vakkali saw IT as he stood at the edge of the cliff with one foot in the air. He saw the Buddha's whole body. (This is a marvelously deep description.) As Vakkali stood with one foot on each side—entity and non-entity—he suddenly saw Reality. He saw, not the physical body, but the Reality of Buddha. He opened the eye of the Mind, and saw the complete body of Buddha, saw the thirty-three signs of Buddha. Before that, he had seen only thirty-two. But in that moment, he saw the concealed sign as well. I think that it is in such a moment that one sees Reality—"Buddha" by name.

This description is metaphorical, of course. Vakkali's mind was dualistic—matter and spirit—one side phenomenal, the other noumenal. But in that moment he saw something that is neither—Reality. Sometimes I don't really like the word "reality," because Transcendentalists use it, but in that moment, Vakkali saw it, and realized it—*Ahhhhh!*

He realized that Buddha had saved him. He had entered Buddhism. It is something like that when one enters the initial part of Zen, as, after passing two or three koans, you realize oneness. It is really the gate of Buddhism. Neither matter nor spirit—just oneness. The entrance is not the sanctuary; there is distance between the entrance and the sanctuary. Vakkali entered JUST THIS. The description is quite symbolic, quite beautiful, and poetic. With one foot in the air, the other on the cliff— suddenly—he saw the Buddha's complete appearance.

But Vakkali was unfortunate. Very soon after this happened, he fell ill. There was a dreadful pain in his breast, and he couldn't eat anything; the pain was killing him. It came upon him one day when he was begging alms in the town of Rajagriha as he was standing in front of the house of a townsman. Suddenly, he felt a terrific stroke of pain, and he fell down and was in agony day and night after that. A nun, who name was Punya [95], happened to see this and felt she had to help him. She nursed him for three months, and for all that time he tossed in agony. Finally, he said to her, "I have not seen my Buddha for three months. I cannot bear this pain much longer. I am going to commit suicide, but before I do, I wish to see my Lord once more. Go, Punya, I beg you, go to the Buddha and ask for his sympathy!"

Punya went to the Buddha and gave him the message from Vakkali. After the Buddha heard about Vakkali he went to see him at the house of a potter where he had been staying. There the Buddha saw him tossing and moaning in great agony. When Vakkali saw the Buddha approach him, he tried to raise up his body. The Buddha said, "Don't try to get up, Vakkali," and he took a seat beside him and asked him a question. "Vakkali," he asked, "Do you think this body is eternal?" (I'm not sure the Buddha would have asked such a question at such a moment, but this is how it is written.)

Vakkali answered, "No, my Lokanatha, this body is ephemeral. It is like a cloud in the blue sky that exists for a little while, then dissolves and disappears into the blue. This is transitoriness."

The Buddha said, "Yes, Vakkali, this is transitoriness, and transitoriness is agony." Vakkali agreed with the Buddha. "Yes, my Lokanatha, this transitoriness of the body is agony. This body is mutable, changeable. From one moment to the next it changes appearance, but I do not trust this body."

The Buddha said, "If you attain non-ego, you will see eternal emptiness. If you transmute yourself into eternal emptiness, and from that standpoint observe this transitoriness, you will find non-ego. Attaining non-ego, you will find that your pain is not pain and that it is not yours." (I think when my students hear this they will understand from their experience with the koan about the agony of death [96].)

Vakkali said, "I have heard your teaching many times, but please tell me how I can escape from this pain, this agony. If you will permit me, I will cut my throat with my dagger and take leave of this transitory body."

The Buddha replied no word to this, but turned on his heel and went back to Eagle Mountain.

That midnight two *devas*, one male and one female, appeared to the Buddha. One said, "Vakkali decided to commit suicide." The other said, "He will emancipate himself from agony." Then both, trailing their long robes, disappeared into the sky, leaving no trace. It was like a dream. You must understand that this description is of the Buddha's thoughts.

The next morning the Buddha asked his disciples to go down the mountain. Near the entrance to Shravasti was the Black Stone Grotto. He had told his disciples about the two *devas* and felt that something had happened. The disciples went to the potter's house to see Vakkali.

The previous night Vakkali had asked Punya to leave. He told her that he was going to commit suicide. "Do not tell anyone," he said. "But ask the members of this family to carry me to the Black Stone Grotto. I will commit suicide there, as I do not wish to die in a layman's house."

The Black Stone Grotto was an ill-omened place to Buddhists. It had been occupied by the Naked Sect, the Jains, but after the Buddha's sect came to dominance, the Jains left it. It was so dark and unpleasant, no one liked to go there to meditate; it was like a place of sickness. Later on it was the place where the heretics killed Maudgalaputra, a great disciple of the Buddha, by rolling a huge stone upon him. Supported by a cane, his body bruised and his bones broken, he reached the gate of Shariputra—another disciple of the Buddha—called Shariputra's name, and died there.

When Vakkali reached the Black Stone Grotto, he asked the laymen who had carried him there to go back home. Then he took his dagger, cut into the most painful part of his breast, and died. In the morning the Buddha, attended by his disciples, went to find him. Entering the grotto the Buddha saw his body and turned his head away. They had found him bathed in blood. His black hair was his shroud. All the disciples were afraid, and none approached the corpse. Scarcely looking at it, they circled it and turned their faces away.

The Buddha said, "Look at the black hair around him. The mist touched his body and changed it into dust. Vakkali does not look like a *bhikshu* anymore. He looks like a demon. Killing himself, he has turned himself into a demon."

The disciples asked the Buddha, "Where is his consciousness now, Lokanatha?"

The Buddha said, "He killed his consciousness with his dagger, so his consciousness is not living anymore."

Vakkali committed suicide before he really attained true understanding. His understanding was that Consciousness is the center of the universe. When you come into Buddhism, you strike your breast and say, "This is the center."

What does this mean?

Vakkali took his dagger and struck his breast and died. Do you think he thought his consciousness was in his heart?

An *arhat*, in his dying moment, attains nirvana if he goes into bottomless nothingness. But when his body suddenly goes into bottomless nothingness in his meditation, he feels fear. He thinks, "I cannot attain nirvana if I go into this bottomless nothingness."

In many religions God is Consciousness. Consciousness in the sky, or Consciousness in the universe, they search for a Consciousness center somewhere. When you are depending upon your own consciousness as you are dying and feel your consciousness scattering, you shriek as you see that bottomless emptiness. You think you are falling. You are afraid, and you are in agony. It was the same with Vakkali. It's a disgraceful death that you are dying. One who believes that Consciousness is the center always meets this fear when dying.

Vakkali was meditating when he was in agony and thought he could not concentrate into his consciousness. His willpower relinquished consciousness. When he looked into bottomless hell, into nothingness, and felt that his consciousness would disappear, he thought he could still hold onto his consciousness, and use a dagger and be reborn into another state. It was his hope that before his consciousness disappeared, he would leave his body with that consciousness. So he killed himself in order to retain his consciousness and go with it to another body. This was his mistake. He thought to escape agony. But he was dead before he attained Buddhism. The Buddha said Vaikkali's consciousness was not living anymore. He killed it with his dagger.

# COMPENSATION

In the early sutras the Buddha's teachings are described in the form of memoranda. This morning's lecture, given by the Buddha to his young monks, has the genuine sound of the Buddha's own words. When we read these words we realize this was not a lecture given by one of the Buddha's disciples. In this sutra, the human quality of the Buddha is tangible.

> *Therefore, O monks, you should learn this lesson: You must know the other's kindness and must requite it. You must requite even a small kindness, to say nothing of a great kindness.*

The other's kindness is Buddha's kindness. In the Zen view this is the manifestation of All-Law. Buddha is your original nature. To requite the kindness of Buddha means to realize your own original nature and understand the Law.

In Buddhism the teacher makes disciples. The disciples carry the teacher's teaching and give it to their own disciples. This is requiting. Though you give the teacher food, clothing to wear, a house to live in, this does not mean you are requiting the teacher's kindness. You must attain enlightenment yourself and accept the teacher's Dharma and then pass it on to your followers. In Buddhism this is called compensation. It a bond of filial piety between teacher and disciple.

Sometimes, however, it happens in the Zen room that a student thinks: My *roshi* never passes me on my koan because I did not make a donation! There is no such *roshi* in Zen. To pass the koan accepting the teacher's view is paying your debt to the teacher more than giving one hundred dollars.

Zen teaching is very simple. In the first stage you are deluded; you are in original darkness; you don't know where you are; you don't know what it is all about. This is the first stage. The second stage is when you realize what your original nature is, what the true state of Reality is. To attain this stage many young monks in ancient days obeyed very severe commandments, renounced the world, and lived ascetic lives, purifying their minds and bodies, concentrating on that state called Reality with body, mind and soul, and attaining it. The third stage is reached when you have attained the state of Reality and move into it. In Buddhist terms, you think about it, you offer your prayers to be born in that state, and then you are born in it. But when you move into it, you cannot call it the "state of Reality" anymore— it is Pure Existence, True Emptiness. There is no "emptiness" left in that state, and you refuse nothing in that state.

In the fourth stage you come back again. But when you come back again it will not be to a place of delusion any more. Then the pure force of Emptiness performs its agency in this world—you are enlightened. Therefore, you see the Law. In the *Sutra of Perfect Awakening* this stage is expressed as "marvelous existence." The flower is not the usual flower, the moon is not the usual moon, the willow is not the usual willow; but the flower is red, the willow is green and the moon is shining. This is the whole teaching of Buddhism, and of Zen, too.

I carry this teaching into America. Its principle is this True Emptiness. This True Emptiness is the principle of Buddhism, the so-called purpose of Bodhidharma's coming from the West. What is that purpose? No purpose. It is like the man in the treetop, holding on to the branch with his teeth, his hands and feet dangling in the air. Someone below asks him, "What is the purpose of Bodhidharma's coming from the West?" And the man in the treetop must answer. Biting the tree branch, how can he answer? If he answers a word he will fall [97].

The purpose of Bodhidharma is the true principle of Buddhism. The main principle of Buddhism is not the words "True Emptiness."

You must grasp it, not merely utter its name. You must realize this True Emptiness, and then change your attitude and manifest yourself thus in this world.

I carry this message to the West. It is my mission. To give this message to America is my purpose. There are many philosophies in the West talking about Reality, but their message is not complete. They never return from there. I brought this complete teaching from the East. Even in Japan many monks attain just one side. I began to study Zen at an early age. At forty-eight I completed the hairpin turn of Buddhism.

I came to America this last time in 1928, on August 16th, when I landed in Seattle, Washington. I have stayed ten years. On the first day I began to make a hermitage. Everyone helped me. Everyone fought against invisible enemies. Those who will be converted to Zen in the future are our enemies. We are fighting against them to capture them. Many have been wounded and dropped out of the lines, but all those people who helped have left mementos that are still vivid in this temple. Their footprints are everywhere and their bloodstains are left, and I am grateful to them.

I have reached the point where I have dug a trench and embanked it and made a foothold. I have worked for ten years, and my friends helped me, and I shall be working for another ten years. I am not doing this for my own purpose; I would be happier in Japan working with my own people. But I love this country, and have decided to die in this country. Eastern civilization must be brought here; we have been misunderstood. I shall die here, clearing up debris to sow seed. It is not the time for Zen yet. But I am the first of the Zen School to come to New York and bring the teaching. I will not see the end.

# THE NIRVANA OF THE BUDDHA

The Buddha lived eighty years, and taught his disciples for over forty years [98]. He left home when he was twenty-nine and attained the highest wisdom after six years of meditation. The number of his monks and nuns was twenty-five hundred, and there were also lay followers. In his lifetime, his teachings were promulgated throughout the valley of the Ganges River. Two hundred years after his death, they were promulgated eastward to Ceylon, Burma, and Siam, and then northward to Kashmir and Turkestan. Westward, they were promulgated to Syria and Alexandria. The Buddha's disciples were also in Athens. Five hundred years after his nirvana, Buddhism reached China and then Korea, and from Korea to Japan. Buddhism is the oldest and greatest religion still existing on earth, and it is still living. Twenty-five hundred years ago the Buddha revealed his nirvana to us.

When your father dies, and you see him in his casket, you see him in nirvana. You see that he resting in another state. He does not speak to you. He does not smile at you. He is in the depths of something your naked eye can actually see, your fingertip feel, your eye fathom, and your ear hear. It is your intuition that knows that immobile and infinite state. But, alas, your mind cannot reach there.

At the time of the Buddha's death, his disciples were divided into five groups—five hundred to a group. Some were staying in the Bamboo Garden, others on Eagle Mountain, and so on. Mahakasyapa, one of the Buddha's chief disciples, was staying with a group of five hundred that were about 120 miles from where the Buddha was. One night, one of the monks in his group had a dreadful dream, and in the morning he told Mahakasyapa about it: "Light filled my cave," he said, "and blossoms fell from heaven. This must be a sign of the Buddha's death. We must go to see him at once."

With their bowls in one hand and their staffs in the other, they all hurried off to Kushinagara Castle, where the Buddha was staying, walking day and night. Mahakasyapa, who was then an old man, about the same age as the Buddha, was carried by the monks.

On the way, they met a student of the Naked Sect, a Jain, carrying a white flower—obviously not an earthly flower, but a heavenly flower—and Mahakasyapa asked, "Where have you come from, and where did you get that flower?"

The Jain answered, "I saw the Buddha enter nirvana seven days ago; *apsaras* [99] and *devas* were offering incense and flowers to him. This is one of those flowers I brought along with me."

When Mahakasyapa heard that the Buddha was indeed dead, he threw himself upon the ground and wept. The monks who were with him also wept. "O Tathagata!" they cried, "Why did you stay so short a time on earth? You came only yesterday, and now, before we have enlightened ourselves, you have left us! Why, Enlightened One, Light of the World? Why did you vanish?"

And they beat their chests and crawled upon the ground.

Finally they came to the gate of Kushinagara Castle, and Ananda was waiting for them. Seeing Mahakasyapa, he flung himself into his arms and wailed. He cried as the injured child throws himself into his mother's lap. But then an old monk came forward and said to them, "Stop crying! While the Buddha was living he was always telling us not to do this and not to do that. Now we can do anything we want!"

At this point, a *deva* is reported to have heard the old monk's words and tried to strike him down, but Mahakasyapa held the *deva's* arm. Then Mahakasyapa said, "Old monk, we lost everything. Now that he is gone, we have nothing to rely upon. All are weeping, and you are happy, but you are happy because you are an idiot."

But when the monk heard the words of Mahakasyapa, the bottom of his mind fell away, and he attained enlightenment. (Of course, the meaning of this story is deep, and that is why it is used as a koan. The monk was not an idiot. When Mahakasyapa pointed out to him the truth of the matter with profound understanding, the monk became enlightened.)

As this was going on, the citizens of Kusinagara, the Mallas, had finished preparing the Buddha for cremation. According to some descriptions, the Buddha's body had been washed in perfumed water and then wrapped in cloth. Round and round he was covered, from his shoulders to his feet. Then he was laid in a golden casket, and the golden casket was placed in an iron casket, and the iron casket placed in a sandalwood casket. Then flowers and scented bark were placed on top, and the threefold casket was placed on a funeral pyre.

Holding a torch, a young leader of the Mallas tried to start the Buddha's pyre burning, but it would not catch fire, so his father took the torch and tried again. But each time the fire caught, it was immediately extinguished. This happened three times. Then a monk by the name of Aniruddha said, "Stop! The Buddha cannot be burned by a fire kindled by man."

It was at that moment that Mahakasyapa and the five hundred monks arrived. Wading the Great River, they swept up the shore like a flood and dashed toward the pyre, and as they circled the Buddha's coffin they blew sad tones from their horns of seashell and recited the Buddha's favorite sutras. Three times they circled the Buddha's pyre.

Then Mahakasyapa asked Ananda, "May we see the Buddha once more before we cremate him?" But Ananda said, "No, Mahakasyapa, he is in a threefold casket." Mahakasyapa asked three times, and three times Ananda refused him.

(The threefold casket, of course, is a symbol of the Buddha's three bodies. The outer casket, made of sandalwood, is his body of transformation, his *nirmanakaya*. It is earth. The middle casket, made of iron, is his body of soul, his *sambhogakaya*. It is fire. And the inner casket, made of gold, is his omnipresent body, his *dharmakaya*. It is ether. But the Buddha is not in these three bodies. He is in nirvana, so Ananda said, "You cannot see him.")

Mahakasyapa turned his head to the Buddha's coffin, the caskets opened, and the Buddha showed Mahakasyapa his feet. Clasping the

Buddha's feet, Mahakasyapa pressed them to his brow [100].While Mahakasyapa was reciting a *gatha* [101] before the Buddha's casket, fire suddenly burst from the Buddha's heart, burned through the casket, and kindled the pyre. But then it began to spread in every direction, and no one knew how to stop it. The fire found no boundary. The multitude, disconcerted, began shouting for water, but then Aniruddha said, "Stop. Do not worry. The fire will naturally cease." Then the trees surrounding the pyre shed their leaves upon it, and the fire stopped.

This story is a teaching. The Buddha cannot be burned by a fire kindled by man, but must himself kindle a fire from his heart of nirvana. The gold, the iron, the sandalwood—all existences—were burned by the fire which annihilates all, making the world into one existence. This means *you*, standing in *dharmakaya*, can consume everything—the golden casket, the iron casket, and the fragrant wooden casket.

The Buddha is now in that state. To the Buddhist, nirvana is *existing* Buddha. When we take refuge in Buddha, it is the Buddha who is in the state that is not imagination, not hypothesis, not theory, but *actual* fact. We know he is *here*, in nirvana, and that the enlightened mind *directly* reaches there and knows that state. Your eye can see him, your ear can hear him, and your hand can touch him. But to the unenlightened mind, he is remote and distant. You think he was living twenty-five hundred years ago and not existing here because you cannot see him, or hear him, and your hand cannot touch him. But nirvana is very clear, though it is very mysterious.

# THE SUMMIT

Thus Come, Tathagata, is the name of all Buddhas, past or future. Tathagata came exactly as THAT, and this THAT we never explain. Of course, it is not necessary to explain it. It is the axiom of existence. You will not deny that you exist, that you are living here now. If there is any truth in the universe, this experience is real. But when you think, you do not know.

I have purpose when I take water and food, and I have purpose when I move my arm. But who digests the food? I digest it. But while I am doing it, I do not know. You may cover your eye, but you cannot help reflecting the skin placed upon it. You may stop the mind awhile, but you cannot stop dreaming. It comes without intention. All is one universal power. You can call it Selfhood, but it has no ego. This is not myself, not yourself. Then who is it? This is the first question of all thinkers. To have an answer, you must enter into your own consciousness. Then what is consciousness?

The first gate is *samaya* [102], to enter and receive everything at once upon your mind, hear all sound at once, think all at once, and think nothing. Do not bend to any particular object. Realize that the mind has rhythm, and know how the mind travels swiftly from one point to another. There are many kinds of *samadhi* in this *samaya*. When you concentrate yourself subjectively in *samadhi*, then it is called *dhyana*. This is the Zen way. By this emphasis upon *dhyana*, we tear the film away between this and that. This is religious existence.

I am the son of a Shinto priest. In Shintoism, we worship the gods or *kami*. The god was there when I came to myself with my own soul and mind. I never had any doubt I was with God always, never felt anything between me and God.

My father died when I was fifteen. Before his death, I went to the shrine and offered a prayer to save him by bringing sacred water for him to drink. When I offered my prayer, I felt a wall between me and God. Should I offer this prayer for my father's life? I had doubt. I realized I was not with the *kami*. So I tried to tear down the wall, to enter into the bosom of God. But it was in vain.

This experience, this delusion, was quite strong, and I longed to enter once more. I became a Buddhist. My knowledge was growing, and I, a skeptic, wanted to conquer this doubt. I was suffering, so I entered into Buddhism in order to conquer my doubt—philosophically. When I was twenty-two—in that spring—I once more entered into the bosom of the *kami*.

Whenever I worship an image—a sky, a pebble, a stone, or even my own heart—I always feel that all religious people in all religions have this experience. So it is not necessary to talk philosophy. We feel happiness because we know our own place; we know we are in the bosom of the great Infinite, so we do not give it a name. You may go there through the road of Christianity, I through the path of Buddhism. The one who takes the path of Shintoism just worships. In Shintoism there is no theory, no word of teaching.

All religion is nothing but a path, a way to reach the summit. You can reach the summit from many directions. So there are no two truths in the universe. Reaching the summit, you will be Buddhist, a Christian, etc. Meditation is not the only way, but it is certainly the best way to reach the summit of religious experience. Your own consciousness is Tathagata.

# TRUE RELIGION

When we have true religion, we take refuge in the *dharmakaya*; we have a foundation in the *dharmakaya*. We do not hold any thought, any thing in our minds when we confront the *dharmakaya* and take refuge in it. Without this foundation, we would not have much meaning in our life.

In every moment of our lives, whatever we do, we must have this bottomless truth. Then we can concentrate on our work of the moment. When you eat, why do you cover the table with a cloth and arrange all those pieces of silver in special ways? You do not know it, but it is religion.

We must have this one thing which is the foundation. If anyone were to ask me, "What is religion?" I would say, "My daily life is religion."

# NOTES & GLOSSARY

# NOTES

1. Lin-chi I-Hsuan (*d.* 866); Chinese Zen master during the T'ang dynasty. The *Record of Lin-chi* records his teachings.
2. Sokei-an and Ruth Fuller Everett were married in 1944. In 1958 Ruth Sasaki was appointed priest of the Rinzai Zen temple Ryosen-an, a subtemple of Daitokuji in Kyoto. At Ryosen-an she was given permission to open the First Zen Institute of America in Japan for Westerners who wished to study Zen.
3. *Cat's Yawn* (New York: The First Zen Institute of America, 1947), p.19.
4. Ibid., p. 3.
5. Unpublished commentary on the *Sutra of Perfect Awakening (Yuan-chueh ching)* a Chinese "apocryphal" text purported to have been translated into Chinese from Sanskrit by Buddhatrata in 693.
6. Unpublished notes on Sokei-an by Ruth Fuller Sasaki.
7. According to some notes found in the Institute's archives, Sokei-an had apparently moved with his family to Medford and then to Seattle after Sokatsu's return to Japan. During the summers he walked through Oregon, Washington, and Montana. In winter, he had an arrangement with Tome to take care of the children.
8. *Cat's Yawn*, page 23.
9. "Excerpts from Our Lineage" by Shigetsu Sasaki Roshi, with comments by Ruth Fuller Sasaki and Gary Snyder, in *Wind Bell* (Zen Center of San Francisco), Volume VIII, Number 102 (Fall 1969), page 13. The "excerpts" of the title were taken from *Cat's Yawn*.
10. A *koji* (J.) is a Buddhist layman. In a 1932 letter to the American Buddhist Dwight Goddard, Sokei-an explains the origin of his names Shigetsu and Sokei-an:

    Anja *means the laborer in the temple, one who polishes the rice, or picks up the kindling wood from the mountain, or brings water from the pool, or does all the hard labor for the monks. He is not of the same rank as a monk but lives in the temple community, observing the same commandments as does the*

*novice....Until I was ordained as a Zen master, I was an anja,*
*so I called myself Anja Shigetsu. Shigetsu is the name my*
*teacher gave me as a Zen novice. Shi is 'to point out with [the]*
*finger'; getsu means moon. 'To point out the moon' means a*
*sutra, because a sutra points out the moon of the soul, but no*
*one sees a moon but sees a finger, just as when pointing out food*
*to a dog, he sees not the food but your finger. I was talking the*
*philosophy of Buddhism very seriously but did not know the*
*moon of the soul to which the philosophy was pointing, so my*
*teacher called me 'moon pointer who does not know to what he*
*is pointing.' When I was ordained, he said, 'After all, that blind*
*finger was a moon.' Sokei-an is the name of my hermitage that*
*I am supposed to have—given by my teacher to me as an*
*ordained one. An means hermitage. Sokei [Ts'ao-ch'i] is the*
*name of a place in which the Sixth Patriarch of China was liv-*
*ing. There are not many anjas who have become ordained Zen*
*Masters, [though] there were several in the lineage of the Zen*
*torchbearers. But an anja like myself, holding the reflection of*
*the moon, ordained as Zen master and striving not to lose it, is*
*an omen of the decline of Zen in the Orient—alas!"*

Sokei-an's full Dharma name is Sokei-an Soshin Taiko Choro Zenji.
"Sokei-an" was given to him by his teacher Sokatsu Shaku when he com-
pleted his study of Zen and was given permission to teach. "Soshin" was
given to him by Daitokuji when he became a member of that temple.
"Taiko Choro Zenji" was the name and title conferred upon him by
Daitokuji.

11. *Zen Notes*, Volume XXVII, Number 7 (July 1981).
12. Ibid.
13. *Cat's Yawn*, page 23.
14. Ruth is referring the articles he wrote from 1920 to 1927 for *Chuo Koron*,
a monthly magazine published in Tokyo. In the following decades,
Sokei-an also wrote several pieces for various Japanese-American maga-
zines in the Seattle area. His comments on American culture, as well as
the increasing political tension between Japan and the United States,
would later lead to an intense investigation by the FBI that would cul-
minate in his detention, along with 100,000 other Japanese-American
citizens and resident aliens, as an enemy of the United States.

15. *Wind Bell*, page 14.
16. In Chapter III of his commentary on the *Platform Sutra of the Sixth Patriarch*, Sokei-an said: "When I began my business, I took the attitude of the Sixth Patriarch. The house was the important thing. So I had a house, a chair, an altar, and a pebble-stone. At first I worshipped that. So I began. I just came here, took off my hat, sat down on a chair, and began to speak of Buddhism. That is all." A pebble, according to Sokei-an, "expressed the mystery of the world in a way that no man-made statue could match. The pebble speaks the entire history of the world." "Original Nature: Zen Comments on the Sixth Patriarch's *Platform Sutra*." (Unpublished manuscript.)
17. Unpublished notes on Sokei-an by Edna Fenton.
18. A monk who has quieted his mind and passions.
19. Unpublished notes on Sokei-an by Mary Farkas.
20. See Mary Farkas's introduction and appendix in *The Zen Eye* for more details on Sokei-an and the Buddhist Society.
21. Unpublished commentary on the *Record of Lin-chi*.
22. *Wind Bell*, page 15.
23. Unpublished letter, archives of the First Zen Institute.
24. Unpublished notes on Sokei-an by Ruth Fuller Sasaki.
25. Unpublished notes on Sokei-an by Mary Farkas.
26. *Zen Notes*, Vol. VIII, No. 10, October 1961.
27. See Case 60, "Iron Grinder, The Cow," in *Book of Serenity* (Hudson, Lindisfarne Press, 1990), translated by Thomas Cleary, p. 253.
28. *Ananda and Maha-Kasyapa. From the Chinese Version of the Sutras of Buddhism.* Sokei-ann [sic] Sasaki, trans. (New York: C.M. Neumann: 1931).
29. Letter dated February 15, 1961.
30. Unpublished commentary on the *Record of Lin-chi*.
31. The essential mind of Buddha. Elsewhere Sokei-an said, "*Dhyana-yoga* is what I always do before my lectures. But we do not need to call it by any name. The transparent and clear mind immediately leads you to your original nature, while thinking something deviates you." A comment by Edward Conze in his translation of the *Diamond Sutra* in regard to the Buddha's preliminary disposition before speaking to his disciples is worth noting here: "Preparatory to entering into trance, the Buddha fixes his attention on the breath which is in front of him. He

then enters into a trance which is described in the larger *Prajnaparamita Sutras* as the 'king of all *samadhis*,' and which miraculously persists throughout the preaching of the *Sutra*." *Buddhist Wisdom Books* (London: George Allen & Unwin, 1958), p. 22.

32. This passgae is taken from Sokei-an's lecture in this volume, "The Four Realms of Arupadhatu."

33. Refers to a line from *The Record of Lin-chi*: "A moment of doubt that pervades your mind is earth." Sokei-an's commentary was: "You feel something like a lump of clay in your breast and you cannot eat or digest." (Unpublished manuscript.)

34. Hui-neng (683–718); Chinese Zen master during the T'ang dynasty. The *Platform Sutra of the Sixth Patriarch* records his biography and teachings.

35. As opposed to *yu-wei* (*samskrita*), "doing something."

36. *Dharma* has many meanings, according to context, including "universal principle," "teaching," "thing," "phenomenon," and "mental content."

37. Sokei-an was actually born on March 15. He changed the date of his birth to coinside with the founding of the First Zen Institute of America (formerly the Buddhist Society of America) on February 15, 1930.

38. Ikkyu Sojun (1393–1481); a famed and eccentric Japanese Zen master of the late middle ages, was abbot of Daitokuji, or "Great Virtue" Monastery, founded in 1327 by Zen Master Daito Kokushi (1282–1338).

39. Bodhidharma (d.?) is said to have arrived in China during the reign of Emperor Wu Ti of the Liang (r. 502–49); he is traditionally regarded as the Twenty-Eighth Patriarch or successor in the Indian lineage to Shakyamuni Buddha and the First Patriarch and founder of Ch'an (Zen) in China.

40. Mataichi Miya (n.d.)was an original founder of the Buddhist Society of America and a devoted friend and student of Sokei-an.

41. A "solitary enlightened one"; a disciple of the Buddha who has gained nirvana due to insight into the twelve causes or links (*nidanas*) in the chain of existence. The twelve links, *nidanas*, constitute the chain of dependent origination, *pratitya-samutpada*, in the wheel of *samsara*, the eternal round or transmigration of birth-and-death: 1) *avidya* (ignorance); 2) *samskara* (actions); 3) *vijnana* (consciousness; 4) *namarupa* (name-form); 5) *shadayatana* (six sense realms); 6) *sparsha* (contact); 7) *vedana* (feeling); 8) *tanha* (craving); 9) *upadana* (grasping); 10) *bhava* (becoming); 11) *jati* (birth); 12) *jara-maranamh* (old age and death).

42. Private koan interview with a Zen master.

43. Ether was once believed to be a rarefied element filling space; *akasha* in Sanskrit is space, the container of the great elements.

44. A Japanese sect of Buddhism based on yoga, ancient ritual practices, and philosophy; the "three secrets" of this school, based on body, speech, and mind, are communicated through the use of hand gestures (*mudras*), powerful syllables (*mantras*), and symbolic diagrams (*mandalas*).

45. Japanese and Chinese (Fa-hsiang) sects of Buddhism based on the teachings of the Indian Yogachara school.

46. A sage or saint who has attained release from the cycle of transmigration (*samsara*), the highest state in Hinayana Buddhism.

47. A collection of treatises or sutras that comprise the basic teachings of early Buddhism.

48. These ingrained "habits," termed *bija*, which are described as "seeds" or "germs" (data or impressions of all phenomena), are "stored" in the *alaya-vijnana* during transmigration. Under the influence of *tanha*, craving, and *avidya*, fundamental ignorance, they are "perfumed" in a process referred to as *vasana*. When these seeds or data become active, grow, and mature, they produce fruit, that is, karma. This karma, in turn, produces further karma, thereby sustaining the phenomenal world. It is this process that defiles the *manas*, the source of discrimination and egoism. However, it is through the power of wisdom, *prajna*, as the seed of enlightenment, that the process termed *ashraya-paravritta* ("the righting of the basis"), characterized as a "revulsion" or "turning over"—what Sokei-an calls "the hairpin turn"—can take place in the *alaya-vijnana*, thereby awakening this consciousness to its original nature.

49. I.e. "No!" "A monk once asked Master Joshu, 'Has a dog the Buddha Nature or not?' Joshu said, 'Mu!'" See case one, "Joshu's Mu," in *Zen Comments on the Mumonkan* by Zenkei Shibayama, trans. Sumiko Kuko (New York: Harper & Row, 1974), p. 19.

    The *Mumonkan* (J., C. *Wu-men-kuan*, "The Gateless Barrier") is a collection of forty-eight koan compiled in 1268 by the Chinese Zen master Wu-men Hui-k'ai (1183–1260).

50. "A monk once asked Joshu, 'What is the meaning of the patriarch's coming from the West?' Joshu answered, 'The oak tree in the front garden.'" Shibayama, *Zen Comments*, case thirty-seven, "The Oak Tree in the Front Garden," p. 259.

51. A moon-face Buddha lives only for a day and night; a sun-face Buddha for 1,800 years. See case three, "Master Ma is Unwell," in *The Blue Cliff Record*, Volume One, translated by Thomas and J.C. Cleary (Boulder: Shambala, 1977), p. 18. "Great Master Ma was unwell. The temple superintendent asked him, 'Teacher, how has your venerable health been in recent days?' The Great Master said, 'Sun Face Buddha, Moon Face Buddha.'" Ma-tsu Tao-i (J. Baso Doitsu, 709–788) was a celebrated Chinese Zen master of the T'ang dynasty.

    *The Blue Cliff Record* (J. *Hekiganroku*, C. *Pi-yen-lu*), is a collection of one hundred koans compiled in the twelfth century by the Chinese Zen master Yuan-wu K'o-ch'in (1063–1135).

52. Sokei-an is referring to what the early school of Yogachara Buddhism has characterized as the "storehouse consciousness." According to this school, human beings are composed of eight consciousnesses. The first five are those of the senses: seeing, hearing, smelling, touching, and tasting. The sixth is the *mano-vijnana*, the intellectual function: knowing, judging, conceiving. The seventh is the *manas*, the discriminative, calculating consciousness, the cause of egoism (dualism). The eighth is the *alaya-vijnana*, the base of all existence and the source of the other seven. The *amala-vijnana* was considered the ninth consciousness, but was later termed the eighth. Another name for the *alaya-vijnana* is *adana-vijnana*, the "holding" or "maintaining" consciousness.

53. The *manas* is sometimes called the *klista-manas*, the defiled mind. "*Manas* is identified as the source of the sense of "I." It exists astride the conscious and unconscious sectors of mind in general and, seeing the seeds it has stored in the *alaya-vijnana*, mistakes the *alaya* for an inherently existing self. What it fails to understand is that the *alaya* is not a static entity, but a river (*ogha*, "flood") that is constantly in motion. The *alaya* is indeed a self, just as a river is indeed a river, but it is not an eternal, unchanging, or inherently existing self, any more than a river is eternal, unchanging, or inherently existing. The *alaya* exists below the level of conscious mind, which accounts for the feeling that the real "me" is somewhere deep inside, and the fact that I continue to exist even when asleep or unconscious." *The Vision of Buddhism: The Space Under The Tree* (New York: Paragon House, 1989) by Roger J. Corless, pgs. 179–80.

54. I.e., "to be yoked," "harnessed," or "in contact with."

55. I.e., *tanha*, "craving." "*The Sutra of the Turning of the Wheel of the Law* states that the cause of suffering is 'craving that... continually finds pleasure and delight now here, now there.'" See *Essentials of Buddhism: Basic Terminology and Concepts of Buddhist Philosophy and Practice* (Tokyo: Kosei Publishing Co., 1996) by Kogen Mizuno, p.156.

56. The Buddha's "tree of enlightenment" (*Ficus religiosa*), under which he attained complete awakening.

57. *Vimukti* ("deliverance"); *jnana*, ("knowledge" or "wisdom"); *darshana* ("seeing" or "discernment").

58. Supernatural beings mentioned in the *Lotus Sutra*: *devas* (gods or angels), *nagas* (rain dragons), *yakshas* (violent, malignant beings), *gandharvas* (heavenly musicians), *garudas* (birdlike beings), *kinnaras* (musicians like *gandharvas* but of lower rank, with men's bodies and horses' heads), *mahoragas* (dragonlike serpents), and *kumbhandas* (monsters).

59. The "Sutra of the Great Decease," translated by Chu Fa-hu between 265 and 313, purports to be the sermon delivered by the Buddha before his death, or *parinirvana*, the complete nirvana of perfect tranquility.

60. The process of emancipating oneself from evils one by one.

61. "What do you think, Subhuti, is the Tathagata to be seen by means of his possession of marks? Subhuti replied: No indeed, O Lord. The Lord said: If, Subhuti, 18the Tathagata could rerecognized by his possession of marks, then also the universal monarch would be a Tathagata. Therefore the Tathagata is not to be seen by means of his possession of marks. Subhuti then said: As I, O Lord, understand the Lord's teaching, the Tathagata is not to be seen through his possession of marks. Further the Lord taught on that occasion the following stanzas:

> Those who by my form did see me,
> And those who followed me by voice
> Wrong the efforts they engaged in,
> Me those people will not see.

> From the Dharma should one see the Buddhas,
> From the Dharmabodies comes their guidance,
> Yet Dharma's true nature cannot be discerned,
> And no once can be conscious of it as an object.

See Conze, *Buddhist Wisdom Books*, pgs. 62-63.

62. A grove offered to the Buddha as a gift by the wealthy merchant Anatha-pindika after his conversion to the Buddha's Dharma.

63. Powerful sound syllables used in esoteric Buddhism.

64. According to A *Dictionary of Chinese Buddhist Terms* by William E. Soothill (London: Kegan Paul, 1937), *ch'an* (J. Zen) is a transliteration of the Sanskrit word *dhyana*, which originally meant "to level a place for an altar, to sacrifice to the hills... to abdicate... Adopted by Buddhists for... 'meditation, thought, reflection, especially profound and abstract religious contemplation'... It was interpreted as 'getting rid of evil,' etc., later as quiet meditation," p. 459. All sects other than the Dhyana Sect are those "who rely on the written word rather than on the 'inner light,'" p. 256.

65. I.e., external objects.

66. The *Lankavatara Sutra* ("Sutra of the Appearance of the Good Doctrine in [Sri] Lanka") is a celebrated Buddhist text that deals with the teaching of the *alaya-vijnana*. Sokei-an is referring to this passage: "When the nature of relative knowledge and particularisation is fully comprehended, they are able to realise the egolessness of an individual person and external object, and gain an insight into the states of Bodhisattvahood," See *Studies in the Lankavatara Sutra*, by D.T. Suzuki (Boston: Routledge & Kegan Paul, 1930), p. 140.

67. *Vajracchika Prajnaparamita Sutra*; a summary of the *Mahaprajna-paramita Sutra* ("Great Perfection of Wisdom Sutra"); translated into Chinese in 400 C.E. by Kumarajiva (334–413).

68. "Everyone has this fan: throughout the twenty-four hours of the day, they completely obtain its power; why do they not know at all when they are asked? Can you speak?" See Case 91, Cleary, *Blue Cliff Record*, p. 586.

69. *Saddharmapundarika Sutra* ("Sutra of the Lotus of the Wonderful Law" or *Lotus Sutra*); one of the most important sutras of Mahayana Buddhism; historically popular in China and Japan.

70. Compilation of early teachings from the Sarvastivada school of Buddhism, composed in the fifth century C.E. by Vasubandhu. This school believed phenomena are real.

71. "The Enlightened and World Honoured One / Has asked about the best expedients / For those in the Dharma ending age / Who wish from samsara to escape / In their search for Nirvana's heart. / It is best to con-

template on worldly sound." *The Surangama Sutra*, translated by Charles Luk (London: Rider and Company, 1966), p.149.

72. A famous Japanese Zen master (1686–1769) of the Tokugawa period from whom present-day Rinzai (Lin-chi) lines in Japan trace their descent.

73. Not infrequently the catagory of *asura* (titanic demons) is included.

74. Chinese and Japanese sect of Mahayana Buddhism. Hui-yuan (336-416) is tradionally considered its first patriarch. The adherents of the Pure Land school believe Amitabha Buddha will make it possible for them to be reborn in the Western Heaven (Sukhavati, the Pure Land) by faith and the chanting of what is referred to in Chinese as the *nien-fo* (J. *nembutsu*), meaning "thinking of the Buddha." The invocation, Na-mo A-mi-t'o fo (J. *Namu Amida Butsu*), "Adoration to Amitabha Buddha," is to be recited with the lips and recollected in the heart and mind.

75. The Vedas are the oldest teachings of Indian literature.

76. World of death.

77. Malignant, evil spirits.

78. I.e. he has attained to *ashraya-paravritti*, the "revulsion or turning-over which takes place at the basis of consciousness, whereby we are enabled to grasp the inmost truth of all existence, liberating us from the fetters of discrimination." D.T. Suzuki, *Studies in the Lankavatara Sutra*, p. 390.

79. "*Citta* is generally translated as 'thought' but... may better be rendered 'mind.' *Studies in the Lankavatara Sutra*, by D.T. Suzuki, p. 398.

80. "Person" or "substance" that is the bearer of the cycle of transmigration.

81. I.e., the wisdom that has crossed over the sea of *samsara* to nirvana.

82. Two monks were arguing about the movement of a temple banner fluttering in the wind. One monk said it was the wind that was moving; the other said it was the flag that was moving. The Sixth Patriarch, overhearing their conversation, said, "...it is neither the banner nor the wind that is moving; it is only your own mind that moves." See section of the "Records of the Transmission of the Lamp" (*Ching-te ch'uan-teng lu*) devoted to the "biography" of Hui-neng translated by Philip B. Yampolsky in *The Platform Sutra of the Sixth Patriarch*, (New York: Columbia University Press, 1967), p. 80.

83. Short Mahayana sutra considered the gist or essence of the voluminous *Prajnaparamita Sutras*.

84. Eminent British philologist and translator (1823–1900).
85. Founder the Middle Way school of Buddhism (Madhyamika) around the second to third centuries C.E..; author of the *Madhyamaka-karika*.
86. I.e., non-dually.
87. I.e., withour attachment.
88. "Skillful means"; teaching methods.
89. Note Sokei-an's statement in his lecture "*Anapana-Smiriti* (Part 2)," *Zen Notes* XVI-6, June 1969: "European scholars think they are nothing but superstition, because gods appeared and spoke to the Buddha. No! This is Mind that comes and speaks to the Buddha. These *devas* are really the mind of Buddha—the Buddha's own mind is being recognized by the Buddha. In a letter to Ruth Everett, dated July 24, 1942, Sokei-an says: "Dear Miss Everett: To confirm our conversation last Wednesday, I shall write two, three words here theologically. The 'person' can be objectified. But personified theory, which is represented by means of an idol, cannot be the image of the 'person.' He who went through this process of awakening does not worship any idols, and he who understands thus is called 'He who has opened the eyes on an image'; and he can be the one who can consecrate an image. This is the reason that a Mahayanist does not worship an idol with secular concepts."
90. The T'ang-dynasty poet Han-shan Te-ch'ing (n.d.), read Kanzan in Japanese.
91. "Lord of the World"; one of Buddha's ten titles.
92. Literally, "unrecordable."
93. Japanese term of address for a Buddhist priest or abbot.
94. Famous African-American singer and film celebrity (1898–1976).
95. Punya means "blessed virtues."
96. See Case 47, "Tosotsu's Three Barriers," Shibayama, *Zen Comments*, p. 316.
97. See Case 5, "Kyogen's Man Up A Tree," in Shibayama, *Zen Comments*, p. 53.
98. The Buddha was born around 560 B.C.E. and died about 480 B.C.E.
99. Celestial nymphs or goddesses of Indra's heaven.
100. The traditional Indian act of veneration and obeisance practiced by lowering the head onto the feet of the guru (*vandana*).
101. Hymn or chant in metrical form found in the sutras.
102. I.e., coming together, meeting.

# GLOSSARY

*Abhidharma*: early Buddhist discourses on philosophy and psychology.

*adana-vijnana*: the "immaculate" consciousness; sometimes considered the ninth consciousness

*Agama Sutras*: collection of treatises or sutras that comprise the basic teachings of early Buddhism.

*akasha*: infinite space.

*alaya-vijnana*: basic, "storehouse" consciousness; the eighth consciousness.

*amala-vijnana*: pure, immaculate consciousness; once regarded as the ninth consciousness.

**Amida** (J.): see Amitabha.

*Amitabha*: literally, "boundless light"; Buddhaof the Western Heaven or Pure Land called Sukhavati.

**Ananda**: cousin and major disciple of the Buddha; known for having heard and memorized his discourses.

*anasrava*: state of non-leakage or discharge of afflictions and passions from the mind.

*anatman*: no-self.

*arhat*: sage or saint who has attained release from the cycle of transmigration, the highest state in Hinayana Buddhism.

*arupadhatu*: realm of formlessness.

*asamskrita* (J. *mu i*, C, *wu-wei*): "not made and not formed"; doing nothing.

**Ashoka**: an important figure in the history of early Buddhism; ruler of the Maurya kingdom of Northern India (r.272 to 236 B.C.E.).

*asrava*: state of leakage or discharge of afflictions and passions from the mind.

*atman*: self.

**Avalokiteshvara**: Bodhisattva of Compassion.

*Avatamsaka Sutra* (The Flower Garland Sutra): Mahayana text dealing with the doctrine of the "unobstructed interpenetration" of Buddha, mind, and phenomena. Translated into Chinese in the fifth century; principle text of the Hua-yen school of Buddhism.

*avidya*: original darkness; beginingless ignorance.

*avyakrita*: unrecordable.

*ayatana*: the six sense-organs and six sense-objects.

*bija*: germs, seeds, data, or impressions of all phenomena that arise from the *alaya-vijnana*.

*bodhi*: awakening.

*bodhisattva*: an enlightened being who seeks buddhahood for the benefit of others.

*ch'an* (J. Zen): the reading of the Chinese character for *dhyana*, a Sanskrit word meaning meditation or absorption.

*citta*: seat of the intellect.

*devas*: angels or gods.

*dharmadhatu*: "realm of *dharma*," the absolute and physical universe.

*dharmakaya*: "body of *dharma*," the essential mind of Buddha; one of the three bodies of the Buddha.

*dhyana-loka*: locus of meditation.

*dhyana-samadhi* (C. *ch'an-ting*): term embracing the entire fields of meditation, concentration, and abstraction.

*dhyana*: tranquil meditation and contemplation.

**eight consciousnesses** (*parijnana*): 1–5) the five senses 6) *manas* 7) *mano-vijnana*, and 8) *alaya-vijnana*.

**eightfold path** (*marga*): the path leading to the cessation of suffering, consisting of: 1) right view (*samyag-drsthi*); 2) right thought and purpose (*samyak-samkalpa*); 3) right speech (*samyag-vach*); 4) right conduct (*samyak-karmanta*); 5) right livelihood (*samyag-ajiva*); 6) right effort (*samyag-vyayama*); 7) right mindfulness (*samyak-smrti*); 8) right concentration (*samyak-samadhi*).

**eighteen *dhatus***: the six sense-organs, six sense-data, and the six corresponding consciousnesses.

**five *skandhas***: the five "shadows," "scales of consciousness," "aggregates," "heaps," "components" of the human being: 1) *rupa*, the body and outer existence; 2) *vedana*, feelings, perception; 3) *samjna*, conception; 4) *samskara*, mind-elements, mental formations, impulses; 5) *vijnana*, consciousness.

**four great elements**: earth, water, fire, and air.

**four inverted views** (*viparyaya*): 1) immutability (*nitya*), 2) ease (*sukha*), 3) purity (*shuddhi*), and 4) ego (*atman*).

**four noble truths** (*arya-satya*): suffering (*dhukha*); the origin (*samudaya*) of suffering; the cessation (*nirodha*) of suffering; and the path (*marga*) towards the cessation of suffering.

**four wisdoms**: 1) *adarshana-jnana*, "mirror wisdom"; 2) *samata-jnana*, "nondual wisdom"; 3) *pratyaveksana-jnana*, "proper comprehension wisdom"; 4) *krityannusthana-jnana*, "perfect activity wisdom."

**fourfold negation**: 1) all things (*dharmas*) exist; 2) all things do not exist; 3) all things both exist and do not exist; 4) all things neither exist nor do not exist.

**Hakuin Ekaku**: (1686–1769) famous Japanese Zen master of the Tokugawa period from whom present-day Rinzai (Lin-chi) lineages in Japan trace their descent.

**Hinayana**: "small vehicle"; early Buddhism.

**Hosso sect**: an esoteric school of Japanese Buddhism based on yoga, ancient Indian ritual practices, and Buddhist concepts.

*hridaya*: heart, mind, or soul

*jnana*: spiritual knowledge of Reality; an aspect of *prajna* (wisdom).

*kalpa*: incalculable period of time between the creation and recreation of the world.

*kamadhatu*: world of desire, comprising the sensuous desire for food, sleep, and sex.

**karma**: universal law of cause and effect; actions or deeds, themselves born out of past karma, that in turn produce new karma.

*klesha*: defilement, affliction, filth.

**koan** (J., C. *kung-an*): "case" given to students by Zen masters for contemplation or observation.

*loka*: world

**Lokanatha**: "Lord of the World"; one of the Buddha's ten titles.

**Mahayana**: "great vehicle"; later Buddhism.

*mana*: pride, arrogance

*manas*: discriminative and calculating ego consciousness; the sixth consciousness.

*mano-vijnana*: intellectual function of knowing, judging, and conceiving; the seventh consciousness.

*mantra*: powerful sound syllables used in esoteric Buddhism.

*manusya*: human being; one of the six states of existence.

**Mara**: deva symbolizing destruction, murder, and death.

*maya*: phenomenal world of illusion, deception, and hallucination

*mudras*: hand gestures used in esoteric Buddhism.

**Mumonkan** (J., C. *Wu-men-kuan*): "The Gateless Barrier," a collection of forty-eight koans compiled in 1268 by the Chinese Zen master Wu-men Hui-k'ai (1183–1260).

**Nagarjuna**: founder the Madhyamika school of Buddhism around the secondto third centuries C.E.; author of the *Madhyamaka-karika*.

*nagas*: supernatural rain dragons mentioned in the Lotus Sutra.

*naraka*: hell; one of the six states of existence.

*nirmanakaya*: "body of transformation"; one of the three bodies of Buddha.

*nirodha*: cessation, annihilation.

*nitya*: immutability, unchangeableness.

*Osho* (J.): term of address for a Buddhist priest or abbot.

*paramartha*: highest and ultimate truth, Reality.

*paramitas*: perfections practiced by a bodhisattva "to reach the other shore (nirvana)."

*prajna*: intrinsic, transcendental wisdom.

*prajnaparamita*: wisdom that has gone beyond (the phenomenal world).

*pratimoksa*: salvation of releasing oneself from evils one by one.

*pratyeka-buddha*: one who has gained nirvana due to insight into the twelve *nidanas*; a "solitary enlightened one."

*preta*: hungry ghost.

*pudgala*: substance ("person," "soul," or "form") that is the bearer of the cycle of transmigration.

**Pure Land Buddhism**: Chinese and Japanese school of Mahayana Buddhism traditionally founded by its first patriarch, Hui-yuan (336–416).

*raksha*: malignant, evil spirit.

*rupa*: form, body, five senses, outer existence; one of the five *skandhas*.

*rupadhatu*: world of form.

*samadhi*: state of perfect absorption into the object of contemplation, a state of non-dual consciousness.

*samapatti*: a concentrated state of mind.

*sambhogakaya*: "body of bliss"; one of the three bodies of Buddha

*samjna*: conception; one of the five *skandhas*.

*samsara*: eternal round (transmigration) of birth-and-death.

*samskara*: mind-elements, mental formations, impulses; one of the five *skandhas*.

*samskrita* (C. *yu-wei*): "doing something."

*samyag-dristhi*: "right view"; see Eightfold Path.

*sangha*: Buddhist community.

*sanzen* (J.): private koan interview with a Zen master.

*sarvadharma*: "all *dharmas*," all things.

*shila*: precepts followed by monks, nuns, and laymen; constituting one of the six paramitas.

Shingon sect: Japanese form of esoteric Buddhism based on the "three secrets" of body, speech, and mind that are communicated through the use of hand gestures (*mudras*), powerful sound syllables (*mantras*), and symbolic diagrams (*mandalas*).

Shinto: Indigenous religion of Japan, literally, "the Way of the Gods."

*shravakas*: disciples who are only capable of "listening" to the teaching.

*shunyata*: emptiness, nothingness, transparency.

six realms (*sad-gati*): various modes of samsaric existence in which rebirth occurs, consisting of three lower states: 1) *naraka* (hell), 2) *preta* (hungry ghosts), 3) *tiryagyoni* (animals); and three higher: 4) *manusya* (human beings), 5) *asura* (titanic demons), and 6) *deva* (gods or heavenly beings).

*smriti*: mindfulness

sutra: discourse attributed to the Buddha.

Tao: A term derived from the Chinese character for "Way"; used both philosophically, as a form of Chinese hermeticism, and religiously, as a practice devoted to achieving immortality.

Tathagata: "Thus Come," "So Come"; one of the ten titles of Buddha.

ten commandments (precepts): 1) no killing, 2) no stealing, 3) no sexual misconduct, 4) no lying, 5) no use of intoxicants, 6) no gossip, 7) boasting, 8) no envy, 9) no resentment and ill will, and 10) no slandering the three treasures.

three bodies of the Buddha (*trikaya*): *dharmakaya, sambhogakaya, nirmanakaya.*

three worlds (*tridhatu*): *kamadhatu, rupadhatu, arupadhatu.*

three treasures: Buddha, Dharma, Sangha.

three worlds (*tridhatu*): past, present, and future.

*tiryagyoni*: beast, animal; one of the six states of existence in the world of *kamadhatu.*

twelve *nidanas*: causes or links in the chain of existence: 1) old age and death; 2) rebirth; 3) existence; 4) grasping; 5) love, thirst, desire; 6) receiving, perceiving, sensation; 7) touch, contact, feeling; 8) the six senses; 9) name and form; 10) the six forms of perception, awareness or discernment; 11) action, moral conduct; 12) ignorance.

*vasana*: the process of perfuming the seeds (*bija*) in the alayavijnana

*vedana*: feeling; perception; one of the five skandhas.

*vijnana*: consciousness; one of the five skandhas.

*vikalpa-klesha*: distress, pain, and affliction (*klesha*) that arises from false discrimination (*vikalpa*) leading to karmic rebirth.

*vimukti*: liberation implying the "loosing of entanglements."

*viparyaya*: see four-inverted views.

*visaya*: six sense objects.

*yama-loka*: place in hell (*naraka*) sentient beings go to be punished by the assistants of Yama after death.

*yoga*: the "discipline" or "yoke" of contact;. unity

*zazen* (J., C. tso-ch'an): seated meditation.

**Zen** (C. *ch'an*): Japanese pronunciation of Chinese *ch'an*, which is the reading of the Chinese character for *dhyana*, a Sanskrit word meaning meditation or absorption; sect of Buddhism emphasizing meditation as the gateway to enlightenment and liberation.

The "weathermark" identifies this book as a production of Weatherhill, Inc., publishers of fine books on Asia and the Pacific. Editorial supervision, book and cover design: D.S. Noble. Production supervision: Bill Rose. Printing and binding: Quebecor. The typeface used is Electra, with Rotis SemiSerif for display.